The Art of Medicine
in Ancient Egypt

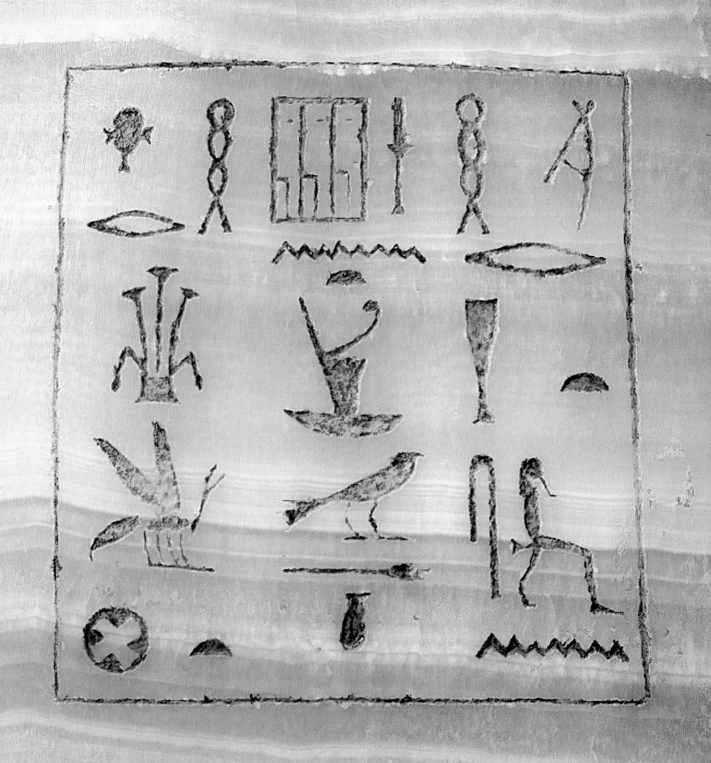

The Art of Medicine
in Ancient Egypt

JAMES P. ALLEN

WITH AN ESSAY BY DAVID T. MININBERG, M.D.

THE METROPOLITAN MUSEUM OF ART, NEW YORK
YALE UNIVERSITY PRESS, NEW HAVEN AND LONDON

This volume has been published in conjunction with the exhibition "The Art of Medicine in Ancient Egypt," held at The Metropolitan Museum of Art, New York, from September 13, 2005, to January 15, 2006.

The exhibition is made possible in part by Raymond and Beverly Sackler.

Additional support for the exhibition and its accompanying catalogue has been provided by The Adelaide Milton de Groot Fund, in memory of the de Groot and Hawley families.

Published by The Metropolitan Museum of Art, New York
John P. O'Neill, Editor in Chief
Dale Tucker, Editor
Robert Weisberg, Designer
Paula Torres, Production
Jean Wagner, Bibliographic Editor

New photography of works in the Metropolitan Museum collection and of the Edwin Smith Papyrus is by Oi-Cheong Lee, The Photograph Studio, The Metropolitan Museum of Art. All other photographs were provided by the owners of the works and are reproduced with their permission; their courtesy is gratefully acknowledged.

Color separations by Professional Graphics, Inc., Rockford, Illinois
Printed and bound by Arnoldo Mondadori, S.p.A., Verona, Italy

Cover illustration: Detail of the Edwin Smith Papyrus (verso, column 5), Dynasty 16–17, ca. 1600 B.C. (see cat. no. 60)
Frontispiece: Detail of Ointment Jar, Dynasty 25, ca. 700 B.C. (see cat. no. 56)

Library of Congress Cataloging-in-Publication Data

Allen, James P., 1945–
    The art of medicine in ancient Egypt / James P. Allen with an essay by David T. Mininberg.
        p.   cm.
    "This volume has been published in conjunction with the exhibition "The art of medicine in ancient Egypt," held at The Metropolitan Museum of Art, New York, from September 13, 2005, to January 15, 2006."
    Includes bibliographical references.
    ISBN 1-58839-170-1 (pbk.) — ISBN 0-300-10728-5 (Yale University Press)
    1. Medicine, Egyptian—Exhibitions. I. Metropolitan Museum of Art (New York, N.Y.) II. Title.
    R137.A55 2005
    610'.74'7471—dc22
                                                    2005016908

CONTENTS

DIRECTOR'S FOREWORD

Great art so often captivates us with its beauty and timelessness that we tend to forget the everyday reality of the lives that produced it. This is especially true for the art of ancient Egypt, since its creators are almost all anonymous. For us, who encounter such treasures millennia after their making, Egyptian art reflects not the vision of a single person but that of an entire civilization. Usually its themes are the lofty ones that invest all great art: nobility, divinity, and the mysteries of life and death. In that long shadow the more mundane concerns are easy to overlook, yet these too found expression in the art created in the ancient Nile Valley.

"The Art of Medicine in Ancient Egypt" illustrates how concern for the preservation and restoration of health influenced Egyptian art. With one exception, the objects in this exhibition were assembled from the permanent collection of The Metropolitan Museum of Art. Although many of them are humble representatives of quotidian life, they bring us closer to their anonymous creators than do the recognized "masterpieces" of Egyptian art. They are eloquent witnesses to the world of ancient Egypt and the minds of those who lived in that world. Complementing them, and forming the centerpiece of the exhibition, is one of the prime documents in the history of human thought, the Edwin Smith Papyrus. Displayed in public for the first time in more than half a century, it has been included by courtesy of the Malloch Rare Book Room of the New York Academy of Medicine. We are grateful to the Academy and its president, Dr. Jeremiah A. Barondess, for the privilege of exhibiting the papyrus and illustrating it in this catalogue.

This exhibition was conceived and organized by James P. Allen, curator in the Metropolitan Museum's Department of Egyptian Art, who also wrote most of the catalogue. We are extremely grateful to Raymond and Beverly Sackler for their crucial assistance toward the realization of this exhibition. We are likewise indebted to The Adelaide Milton de Groot Fund, in memory of the de Groot and Hawley families, for the invaluable support it provided for this exhibition and its accompanying catalogue.

Philippe de Montebello
Director
The Metropolitan Museum of Art

ACKNOWLEDGMENTS

No exhibition is the product of one person alone. "The Art of Medicine in Ancient Egypt" would not have been possible without the active participation of many people whose efforts deserve acknowledgment in addition to my gratitude. I am grateful above all to Dorothea Arnold, Lila Acheson Wallace Chairman of the Department of Egyptian Art, for her enthusiastic support, guidance, and collaboration in every phase of the exhibition. My thanks also go to David T. Mininberg, M.D., the department's medical consultant, for his scientific advice and his invaluable service as liaison with the medical community, and to my colleagues in the department, Diana Craig Patch and Susan J. Allen. All four have also had a hand in the writing of this catalogue.

The exhibition itself was designed by Daniel Bradley Kershaw, with graphic design by Sue Koch and lighting by Clint Ross Coller and Richard Lichte, all members of the Metropolitan Museum's Design Department.

This catalogue was produced by the Museum's Editorial Department, under the direction of John P. O'Neill, Editor in Chief and General Manager of Publications. It was edited by Dale Tucker, designed by Robert Weisberg, and produced by Paula Torres; I am grateful for their patience as well as their care and talent. Photographs for the exhibition and catalogue were taken by Oi-Cheong Lee of the Museum's Photograph Studio.

A special word of thanks is due to the staff of the New York Academy of Medicine for their assistance in making possible the exhibition of the Edwin Smith Papyrus: above all to Miriam Mandelbaum, Curator of Rare Books, and to her colleague Susan B. Martin, Head of the Gladys Brooks Book and Paper Conservation Laboratory. The papyrus was conserved and newly mounted by Akiko Yamazaki-Kleps, in the Metropolitan Museum's Department of Paper Conservation, under the direction of Marjorie Shelley, Sherman Fairchild Conservator in Charge.

James P. Allen
Curator
Department of Egyptian Art

Contributors to the Catalogue

Catalogue entries were written by James P. Allen unless otherwise signed. All of the authors listed below are in the Department of Egyptian Art, The Metropolitan Museum of Art.

JPA
James P. Allen
Curator

SJA
Susan J. Allen
Senior Research Associate

DA
Dorothea Arnold
Lila Acheson Wallace Chair

DCP
Diana Craig Patch
Assistant Curator

DTM
David T. Mininberg, M.D.
Medical Consultant

Note to the Reader

Following standard Egyptological practice, square brackets in translations indicate losses in the original, and parentheses mark modern editorial additions and commentary. All texts in this volume were translated by James P. Allen.

Dimensions of catalogue objects are given in inches followed by centimeters. Unless otherwise noted, height precedes width precedes depth. All catalogue objects are in the Department of Egyptian Art, The Metropolitan Museum of Art, except for the Edwin Smith Papyrus (cat. no. 60), which is courtesy of the Malloch Rare Book Room of the New York Academy of Medicine.

Citations and bibliographies include full references, with the exception of the following abbreviations:

BMMA
Bulletin of the Metropolitan Museum of Art; some issues have title *Metropolitan Museum of Art Bulletin*

Hayes, *Scepter* I
William C. Hayes. *The Scepter of Egypt: A Background for the Study of the Egyptian Antiquities in The Metropolitan Museum of Art*. Part I, *From the Earliest Times to the End of the Middle Kingdom*. Rev. ed. New York: The Metropolitan Museum of Art, 1990. First published New York: Harper & Brothers, 1953.

Hayes, *Scepter* II
William C. Hayes. *The Scepter of Egypt: A Background for the Study of the Egyptian Antiquities in The Metropolitan Museum of Art*. Part II, *The Hyksos Period and the New Kingdom (1675–1080 B.C.)*. Rev. ed. New York: The Metropolitan Museum of Art, 1990. First published Cambridge, Mass.: Harvard University Press, 1957.

MMA
The Metropolitan Museum of Art

MMJ
Metropolitan Museum Journal

The Art of Medicine in Ancient Egypt

James P. Allen

The relics of ancient Egyptian civilization testify to the Egyptians' perpetual efforts to understand and cope with the world they lived in. Egypt's panoply of gods explained the elements and forces that constituted and governed that world: the earth, sky, and sun; the river Nile and its annual, life-giving inundation of the fields; and the institution of kingship, which rebuffed external enemies, quieted internal disorder, and made peaceful life possible. The institutions and ceremonies of Egyptian religion were the means by which those forces were at once appeased and cajoled into acting for the benefit of the Egyptians themselves, in this life and in the next.

These perceptions and themes imbue all ancient Egyptian art, from masterpieces intended to honor the gods and kings to the most prosaic objects of everyday life. For most Egyptians, however, the perpetuation of order in the world and in society was of less immediate concern than the course of their own daily lives—an existence that, although advanced and sophisticated by the standards of its time, was continually hazardous. The Nile, along whose banks most Egyptians lived, was populated by crocodiles and hippopotami; the deserts, never more than a few miles away, were home to lions, hyenas, jackals, scorpions, and snakes; and the arable land, in which Egypt's inhabitants lived and worked, teemed with yet more serpents and dangerous insects. Diseases carried by flies and parasites in the river and irrigation canals presented the constant threat of blindness, disability, and death. Soldiers and men who labored in the stone quarries and on Egypt's massive construction projects risked crippling or mortal injuries, and women often died in childbirth. Life expectancy was short, rarely more than forty years for most Egyptians. Even the elite, who lived in relative ease and often enjoyed a longer life span, could spend their final years in excruciating pain from dental disease.

These threats posed a constant challenge to ancient Egyptian life, but their role in the creation and motifs of Egyptian art has been largely overlooked. This catalogue and the exhibition it illustrates examine the expression of medical concerns in Egyptian art as well as the practice of ancient Egyptian medicine as an art. These two themes of "The Art of Medicine in Ancient Egypt" reflect the Egyptians' own approach to medicine, which was practical and subjective at the same time. Although modern society has separated these two characteristics into the discrete fields of science and art, to the ancient Egyptians they were inseparable; both derive from the single basic concern of dealing with the prevention and cure of illness in the most effective way possible.

Experience and simple observation revealed the causes of many medical problems as well as the most effective way of treating them. Perhaps the clearest reflection of this is preserved in the Edwin Smith Papyrus (cat. no. 60): each of the forty-eight cases on the recto of the papyrus, which discusses injuries or disorders of the head and torso, bears a title beginning with a word that denotes "knowledge gained from practical experience." Nevertheless, the physical causes of many illnesses remained a mystery to the Egyptians. Faced with the need to explain and address the inexplicable, they concluded that such illnesses were the results of inimical forces that, being of supernatural origin, could be countered only with nonphysical means. The eight magic spells on the verso of the Smith Papyrus illustrate this approach. The Egyptians were aware of the difference between observable and supernatural causes — Case 8 of the Smith Papyrus clearly distinguishes between the two — but they also believed that a successful treatment required that both causes be countered. Accordingly, Case 9 of the Smith Papyrus prescribes not only a practical remedy but a magic spell as well.

Egyptian magic relied on the efficacy of the spoken word and on physical association (the latter often called "sympathetic" magic) to achieve a desired effect. The right words could controvert or deflect malign forces, and the use of particularly evocative amulets or substances that had been in contact with such talismans were expected to have a salutory effect. Both beliefs have a basis in common human experience: the use of language to produce a desired reaction in a human audience, and the utilization of holy waters or relics in cultures around the world.

The more than sixty objects described in this catalogue illustrate how these various themes were expressed in Egyptian art. They reflect several basic aspects of Egyptian medicine: prevention, birth and infancy, injuries and their treatment by practical and magical means, and physicians.

PREVENTION

In ancient Egypt, as in all societies, disease prevention began with cleanliness. A bowl from the Predynastic Period (cat. no. 1) is an early example of this theme in Egyptian art, representing both a functional container for water and an archaic example of the hieroglyph 🝿, meaning "clean." The text inscribed on a jar from the Middle Kingdom (cat. no. 2) illustrates the efficacy of water, while an Old Kingdom basin and ewer (cat. no. 3) reflect its importance to Egyptian everyday life. Kohl tubes (cat. nos. 4–6), among the most common objects of daily life, served both a cosmetic and a medicinal purpose. They contained a ground mineral, usually

galena (cat. no. 8), that both men and women applied around the eyes with a small stick (cat. nos. 5, 7), like modern eyeliner. The dark substance helped to reduce the glare of the Egyptian sun and repelled flies, a common source of eye disease and blindness (cat. no. 9).

The god Bes, whose image appears on thirteen objects in the exhibition, embodies one approach to prevention through magic. His gruesome figure was thought to deter the approach of malevolent gods or hostile spirits of the deceased, and for that reason it complements one of the kohl tubes and a kohl stick holder (cat. nos. 6, 7). The god's image could also be worn as an amulet (cat. nos. 10, 13), displayed for protection in the home or elsewhere (cat. no. 11), and beseeched for intercession (cat. no. 12).

Figures of a hippopotamus goddess called Ipi or Taweret ("The Great One") also served as defensive devices. The goddess was particularly protective of women, as illustrated by a hairpin and container (cat. nos. 14, 15). The hippopotamus was one of the deadliest elements of ancient Egyptian life along the Nile, but for that reason it was also thought to be as dangerous to potentially harmful forces as to the Egyptians themselves. The animal's paradoxical nature is reflected on a scarab belonging to a princess of the Middle Kingdom (cat. no. 13); on the bottom of the object the pharaoh is shown killing a hippopotamus (exemplifying his role as protector of his subjects), while on the back, two images of the goddess appear with Bes as guardians of the scarab's wearer. Jewelry, like kohl, had a purpose beyond mere adornment. Two Horus-eye amulets (cat. no. 16), once part of a necklace, evoke a mythological precedent for recovery from damage and thus served as powerful symbols of protection from harm.

BIRTH AND INFANCY

Childbirth was the most perilous point in the life of every Egyptian. The rate of mortality for both mother and child was high, and the Egyptians employed a wide array of practical and magic devices to ensure a successful delivery and infancy. Most objects reflecting these concerns have survived not from the sphere of everyday life but from tombs, where they were deposited to aid the deceased's rebirth into the afterlife. These include the "fish-tail" flint knives commonly used in Predynastic times for cutting the umbilical cord (cat. no. 17), which in later eras were incorporated into the paraphernalia of the funerary ritual and occasionally buried with the deceased in the form of models (cat. no. 18).

Middle Kingdom burials often included crescent-shaped objects known as "magic wands" (cat. nos. 19–22). Decorated with figures of Bes and other protective beings, these were apparently used during life to keep inimical forces away from the newborn and were deposited in tombs to serve the same purpose for the deceased's spirit. In the inscription on the reverse of one of them (cat. no. 20), the figures say: "We have come that we may extend our protection around the healthy child." A baby's feeding cup from the same period is decorated with similar figures (cat. no. 23). Bes and Taweret were also invoked as aids in childbirth (cat. nos. 24, 25); a stela from the New Kingdom reflects this theme in its unusual depiction of Taweret together with the goddess Mut, whose very name means "mother" (cat. no. 26).

The act of nursing was regarded as second in importance only to childbirth. Mothers' milk was understood to be especially beneficial to the newborn, and special jars were designed to hold excess production (cat. nos. 27, 28). Nursing itself was honored as a life-giving act, both in the abstract—represented by an image of Isis and Horus, the prototypical mother and child (cat. no. 29)—and in the real world, as depicted in a statue of a human nurse (cat. no. 30).

INJURIES AND TREATMENT

Many Egyptians who survived the hazards of birth and infancy still had to face threats of serious injury from the world in which they lived. The bodies of those wealthy enough to be mummified sometimes reveal traces of such injuries (cat. no. 31), and their representations occasionally show them as well (cat. no. 32). The Smith Papyrus is a remarkable testament to the effort the ancient Egyptians expended in coping with such physical traumas. A copy of a text originally composed in the Middle Kingdom, the papyrus was written during a period of internecine struggle and warfare and may have been copied to aid a physician in treating battle casualties. Many, if not all, of the wounds the papyrus describes could have been inflicted by the kinds of weapons Egyptian soldiers and their enemies used in combat (cat. nos. 33–38).

Egyptian medicine was a compendium of treatments and prescriptions compiled almost exclusively through trial and error over the course of millennia. Surgery was rare, and dissection was the province of butchers and embalmers; most depictions of internal organs are of cattle and other animals rather than human beings (cat. no. 39). Physicians employed a vast pharmacopoeia of natural substances. Honey (cat. no. 40) was used for its medicinal properties as well as its sweetness, and the juice of pomegranates (cat. nos. 41, 42) served as both an astringent and a delicacy. Water lilies (cat. nos. 43–46) were revered as images of the sun and youth, but the plant itself has analgesic properties and may have been ingested on occasion for that purpose. Egyptian physicians were probably also acquainted with opium, a poppy extract that can be used as a sedative. Distinctive tall-necked vessels that first appeared during the New Kingdom may have held imports of this substance from Asia Minor (cat. nos. 47, 48).

The role of magic in medical treatment is exemplified by the goddess Sekhmet (cat. nos. 49, 50). Like Taweret, she embodied both malign and protective forces; seen as a source of danger from pestilence and the wild animals of the ancient Egyptian desert (represented by her lion-headed image), she could also be invoked to guard against such evils. Physicians, who were trained in magic as well as in practical medicine, were therefore usually priests of

Sekhmet (cat. no. 57), as noted in Case 1 of the Smith Papyrus.

Magic in ancient Egypt was associative. For the Egyptians, even plain water could acquire curative properties merely by coming into contact with appropriately evocative symbols. This theme is reflected in art by two objects from opposite ends of Egypt's pharaonic history. A delicate libation dish of the Predynastic Period (cat. no. 51) incorporates the hieroglyphs for "life force" (a pair of embracing arms) and "life" (the ankh, or crux ansata), so that water poured from it could confer these benefits. The equally exquisite Metternich Stela (cat. no. 52), carved three thousand years later, is literally covered with magic texts and symbols; water poured over the stela was thought to absorb from them both amuletic and salutory qualities. The stela is the finest example of a genre of Egyptian art known as cippi (cat. nos. 53, 54), which depict the god Horus as an infant vanquishing dangerous beasts. The same theme appears on the foot end of a mummy case (cat. no. 55), where the image of two scorpions crushed beneath a pair of sandals magically enabled the deceased to overcome hostile forces in the afterlife.

PHYSICIANS

The title "physician" ($\overrightarrow{\circ}$ *zwnw*), attested throughout most of ancient Egyptian history, is exemplified by a jar of the Twenty-fifth Dynasty, labeled "special ointment," that belonged to a chief physician named Harkhebi (cat. no. 56). Physicians themselves are represented by a statue of the official Yuny (cat. no. 57), who was also a priest of Sekhmet, and by a portrait head of an anonymous priest (cat. no. 58) whose statue served much the same purpose as the Metternich Stela. A statue of Imhotep (cat. no. 59) commemorates an official of the Third Dynasty who was revered as the "patron saint" of Egyptian physicians. The Greeks equated him with their own god of medicine, Asklepios, although ironically there is no evidence that Imhotep himself was a physician. The scribe who wrote the Smith Papyrus may also have practiced medicine, but even if he did not, the text itself was certainly meant to be used by Egyptian physicians. With its combination of practical and magical approaches to healing, the papyrus is an eloquent representative of the science and art of medicine in ancient Egypt.

The Legacy of Ancient Egyptian Medicine

DAVID T. MININBERG, M.D.

Many of the practices followed by today's physicians are legacies of the skills and knowledge gained by ancient Egyptian physicians. Although there are obvious differences in detail, a good number of the underlying principles of contemporary medicine are remarkably similar to their Egyptian antecedents. The modern physician seeks a medical diagnosis of a disease: a physical cause for a specific derangement in the patient. The ancient physician also tried to identify physical causes for the problem at hand, but with far less knowledge and understanding of the human body he was often compelled to diagnose a nonphysical cause: a supernatural, external vector such as an angry god, demon, or spirit. The coexistence of both approaches is nowhere better illustrated than in Case 8 of the Edwin Smith Papyrus (cat. no. 60), which instructs the physician to distinguish a skull fracture, a physical problem, from "something that has entered from the outside . . . the breath of a god from outside, or a dead man, making entry, not something his body has created."

Because his analysis combined objective and supernatural causes, the ancient Egyptian physician was both a medical doctor and a priest (cat. no. 58), and his treatment often combined the practical with the magical (see, for example, Case 9 of the Smith Papyrus). Medical training was actually a specialized branch of scribal education. Indeed, a modern physician would feel quite at home with much of this instruction, which consisted of studying from texts—handwritten documents, such as the Smith Papyrus—under the guidance of a more senior physician. These papyri were themselves made by scribes who were skilled in the advanced writing system of ancient Egypt: a detailed script that made it possible to designate the parts of the body with distinct terms, promoting diagnostic precision and more effective therapy.

Like his present-day counterpart, the ancient physician could choose to specialize. There were specialists for treatment of the eyes, teeth, internal organs, and for women (obstetrics and gynecology) as well as veterinarians. As was the case with other professions in ancient Egypt, medicine was organized hierarchically, with practitioners working under a chief of physicians (cat. no. 57). The Egyptian physicians' source of knowledge about the internal organs is unclear. Embalmers may have shared some of their observations, but it is more likely that anatomic knowledge was derived from veterinary medicine and butchery, since almost all of the hieroglyphic signs for the internal organs depict animal rather than human anatomy (cat. no. 39). Physicians had a rudimentary, somewhat erroneous concept of the circulatory system, believing the heart to be the center from which emanated vessels carrying air and blood to all parts of the body. They also knew about the pulse, which they referred to as the heart "talking," and about abnormal rhythms, attributed to defects in the heart.

Today's physician would find the ancient Egyptian approach to precise diagnosis very familiar. Each of the cases in the Smith Papyrus is presented in a systematic, diagnostic format, including a history ("If you treat a man for . . ."), physical examination ("you have to . . ."), diagnosis ("then you say about him . . ."), and treatment. This stepwise approach to solving the patient's problem is the same method taught in modern medical schools. Egyptian physicians theorized that disease arose not only from supernatural causes but also from an imbalance in a physical substance, *wḥdw,* produced by internal body processes. This idea is analogous to the Greek notion of humors as well as to the hormones known to modern medicine.

The ancient physician used all the modalities at his disposal to treat his patient, including not only surgery and medications but also intervention against supernatural causes by means of magic spells and prayers. Even today, patients will often consult a physician while they also resort to prayer—their own, or that of others on their behalf—and to the use of amulets and talismans. The surgery performed by the Egyptian physician was apparently restricted to the external anatomy: in other words, to trauma, growths, and wounds. This is well illustrated by the Smith Papyrus, which may have served as a textbook for military physicians. Egyptian surgeons used wood splints to stabilize fractures and linen sutures (thread) to perform necessary repairs. The Smith Papyrus also refers to the several stages of wound healing, noting changes in treatment at each stage of the healing process. Honey was liberally prescribed because the Egyptians observed that it helped to dry up a wound and heal it; treatment today also includes substances with osmotic and antibacterial properties.

Like his modern counterpart, the Egyptian practitioner could avail himself of a substantial pharmacopoeia of drugs with which to treat his patients. The ancient preparations were both mineral and botanical (the latter predominantly herbal), and their efficacy is unknown, but the patients believed in them—a significant step on the way to cure. The sophisticated system of drug delivery included ingestion, inhalation, and fumigation, depending on the ailment being treated. Medications were prepared and administered based on a fixed system of dosimetry (the proportion of the components and the frequency of use) that was recorded in the medical papyri. This promoted repetition of the formulae that worked best instead of a reliance on chance, a practice reflected in the comment appended to Prescription 4 of the Smith Papyrus, "(Proved) good a million times."

Preventive medicine, too, played a significant role, as illustrated by the magic spells on the verso of the Smith Papyrus. Water that had passed over a stela inscribed with magic texts was thought to offer protection from the bites of snakes or scorpions (cat. no. 53). This custom, akin to vaccination (i.e., protection from an external threat), is another example of how ancient Egyptian medicine was similar to that of our own time, at least in its approach. The principles at the core of modern medical training—the practices of today's physicians and the armamentarium available to them—all have counterparts or precursors in ancient Egyptian medicine.

CATALOGUE

PREVENTION

1. BOWL WITH HUMAN FEET

Naqada I–early Naqada II, ca. 3900–3650 B.C.
Provenance unknown
Polished red pottery
H. 9.8 cm ($3\frac{7}{8}$ in.); Diam. 13.5 cm ($5\frac{5}{16}$ in.)
Rogers Fund, 1910 (10.176.113)

Although the human feet that support the bowl add a touch of drollness to the vessel's appearance, they were not created solely as a humorous element.[1] This ceramic form should most likely be read as a three-dimensional counterpart of the hieroglyph , meaning "clean."[2] One side of the bowl is higher than the other so that the contents (clean water) could be easily poured out. In pharaonic times water was presented as a libation to the deceased, and this bowl was probably used for that purpose.[3]

DCP

NOTES

1. The earliest examples of footed vessels have been recovered from several strata at Merimda Beni Salama, a site along the margin of the Nile Delta that was an early settlement (4300–4000 B.C.) with burials nearby. See H. Junker, *Vorbericht über die dritte von der Akademie der Wissenschaften in Wien in Verbindung mit dem Egyptiska Museet in Stockhom unternommene Grabung auf der neolithischen Siedelung von Merimde-Benisalâme vom 6. November 1931 bis 20. Januar 1932* (Vienna: Akademie der Wissenschaften, Philosophisch-Historische Klasse, 1932), pp. 69–70, pl. 5; J. Eiwanger, *Merimde-Benisalâme II: Die Funde der mittleren Merimdekultur* (Deutsches Archäologisches Institut, Cairo: Archäologische Veröffentlichungen 51 (Mainz: Von Zabern, 1988), p. 30, pl. 30.
2. H. G. Fischer interpreted the form of this bowl as a representation of the ancient Egyptian hieroglyph , meaning "bring." Both words use a human-footed vessel in the hieroglyph, but the difference is in the orientation of the vessel on top of the feet. In the hieroglyph for "bring" the vessel is upright, while in the glyph meaning "clean" the vessel is tipped and liquid pours to the ground.
3. The earliest anthropomorphic vessels are from the Delta region. In addition to the Metropolitan Museum's example, there are several other Upper Egyptian examples in red polished ware: a shallow bowl from the Museum of Fine Arts, Boston (03.1954), and two red polished-ware bowls of slightly later date (early Naqada II, ca. 3800–3650 B.C.). Of the latter, one is in the Egyptian Museum, Cairo (JE 63181); see M. L. Keimer, "Sur deux vases prédynastiques de

Khozâm," *Annales du Service des Antiquités* 35 (1935), pp. 161–81. The other is in the Royal Ontario Museum, Toronto (900.2.128); see M. Hoffman, in *The First Egyptians*, ed. K. L. Willoughby and E. B. Stanton (Columbia: McKissick Museum, University of South Carolina, 1988), no. 16.

BIBLIOGRAPHY

Hayes, *Scepter* I, p. 17, fig. 8; H. G. Fischer, "The Evolution of Composite Hieroglyphs in Ancient Egypt," *MMJ* 12 (1977), p. 7n19.

2. WATER JAR

Dynasty 12, reign of Amenemhat III, ca. 1830 B.C.
Illahun
Egyptian alabaster
H. 55.8 cm (21 15/16 in.); Diam. 26.7 cm (10 1/2 in.)
Rogers Fund, 1921 (21.2.6)

This vessel was made for Sithathoriunet, a princess or queen of the Middle Kingdom, whose name means "Hathor of Dendera's daughter." It was found in her tomb near the pyramid of Senwosret II (Dynasty 12, ruled ca. 1887–1878 B.C.) at Illahun, where she was buried during the reign of that king's grandson, Amenemhat III. Although intended to hold ritual libations, the jar derives its shape from prototypes in pottery or metal that are known from the Old Kingdom onward. Those used for washing usually had a spout (see cat. no. 3). Water was an important element in burial rituals, which began with cleansing and libation. The hieroglyphic text incised on this jar illustrates the significance the Egyptians attached to these acts:

> *Princess Sithathoriunet, accept these your cool waters from the earth, which beget everything living and all things, for they are what this earth gives—(this earth) that begets everything living and from which everything comes. May you live through them and be restored through them. May you live and be restored through this air that is from it. It shall beget you and you shall emerge alive through everything you might desire. May they be to your good.*

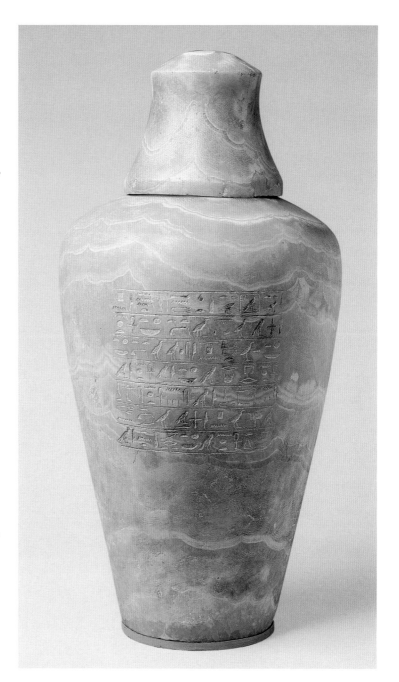

BIBLIOGRAPHY

W. M. F. Petrie, "The British School of Archaeology in Egypt," *Ancient Egypt* 1920, part 3, frontis. and p. 67; W. M. F. Petrie, *Lahun*, vol. 2, Egyptian Research Account 33 (London: British School of Archaeology in Egypt, 1920), pp. 16, 42, pls. 25, 26; Hayes, *Scepter* I, pp. 325–26, fig. 214; C. H. Roehrig, in *The American Discovery of Ancient Egypt*, ed. N. Thomas, exh. cat. (Los Angeles: Los Angeles County Museum of Art, 1995), pp. 151–52.

3. BASIN AND EWER

Dynasty 6, ca. 2200 B.C.
Saqqara, tomb of Tjetju
Copper
Basin: H. 10 cm (3 15/16 in.); Diam. 20 cm (7⅞ in.)
Ewer: H. 11.5 cm (4½ in.); Diam. 11 cm (4 5/16 in.)
Spout: L. 9.8 cm (3⅞ in.); W. 3.5 cm (1⅜ in.); H. 2.5 cm (1 in.) at jar
Rogers Fund, 1926 (26.2.12, 26.2.14)

These two vessels were found in the burial chamber of Tjetju, a vizier of the late Old Kingdom, but they could also have been used by the deceased during life for washing his hands and feet. Their careful workmanship, material, and elegant shapes reflect the importance accorded to cleanliness in Egypt's dusty climate. Tomb chapels and temples were often inscribed with texts admonishing visitors to be clean before entering. In Tjetju's burial chamber, the vessels would have allowed his spirit to cleanse itself before meeting the gods.

BIBLIOGRAPHY

C. M. Firth and B. Gunn, *Teti Pyramid Cemeteries* (Cairo: Institut Français d'Archéologie Orientale, 1926), vol. 1, p. 30, fig. 31; Hayes, *Scepter* I, p. 120, fig. 74; A. Radwan, *Die Kupfer- und Bronzegefässe Ägyptens*, Prähistorische Bronzefunde, Abteilung 12, 2 (Munich: Beck, 1983), p. 59, pl. 27.

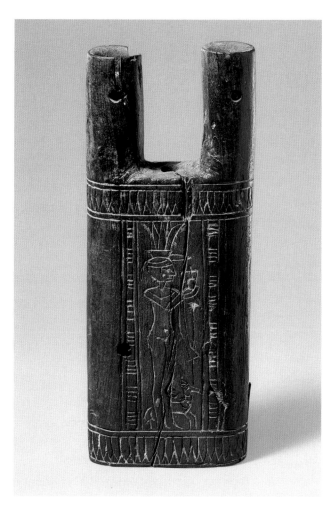

4–5. KOHL TUBES

Dynasty 18–19, ca. 1400–1200 B.C.
Abydos, tomb D 33
Wood
15.9 x 6.2 x 2.5 cm (6¼ x 2⁷⁄₁₆ x 1 in.)
Gift of Egypt Exploration Fund, 1900 (00.4.37)

Dynasty 18, ca. 1400 B.C.
Saqqara
Ebony and ivory
Tube: 7.5 x 5 x 4.5 cm (2¹⁵⁄₁₆ x 1¹⁵⁄₁₆ x 1¾ in.)
Stick: H. 5.1 cm (2 in.); Diam. 0.6 cm (¼ in.)
Rogers Fund, 1926 (26.2.24)

Among the most common remnants of ancient Egyptian daily life, kohl (eye paint) tubes held ground minerals that men and women applied around their eyes for adornment and health. Both malachite and galena were used for this purpose, and most kohl tubes have separate compartments for each mineral. Malachite, which is green, was primarily cosmetic. The black color of galena helped to reflect the glare of the Egyptian sun, and its lead content repelled flies and was deadly to the organisms that can cause eye disease and blindness. The two minerals were ground on slate palettes (see cat. no. 8), mixed with fat, and then applied around the eyes using a small stick, or applicator.

The larger of these tubes (cat. no. 4) is decorated on one side with the image of a young girl and a gazelle and on the other side with a bouquet of flowers, both themes that relate to its cosmetic purposes. The smaller tube, although undecorated, is made of costly ebony and ivory and was found with its applicator.

6. BES KOHL TUBE

Dynasty 18, ca. 1400 B.C.
Provenance unknown
Glazed steatite
6 x 4 x 3.4 cm (2⅜ x 1⁹⁄₁₆ x 1⁵⁄₁₆ in.)
Purchase, Edward S. Harkness Gift, 1926 (26.7.1277)

7. KOHL STICK HOLDER

Dynasty 27, ca. 500 B.C.
Provenance unknown
Faience
9.2 x 4.4 x 3.9 cm (3⅝ x 1¾ x 1½ in.)
Gift of Norbert Schimmel Trust, 1989 (1989.281.94)

Both of these objects, which are separated by nearly a millennium, bear images of the god Bes. One of the more ubiquitous Egyptian deities, Bes served as protector of the home and especially of women and infants. He is usually depicted as a dwarf; his long hair, round ears, and occasional tail derive from early depictions of the god in lion form.

The presence of Bes on these objects reflects the combination of the practical and the magical in Egyptian art. The kohl tube has two compartments, one for green paint and one for black paint. Besides its cosmetic value, eye paint (kohl) was used to prevent diseases of the eye (see cat. nos. 4, 5), repelling flies and other disease-bearing organisms. The Egyptians were unaware of the role these insects played in the transmission of disease, however, ascribing illness instead to the actions of malevolent supernatural forces. The grotesque figure of Bes, sometimes enhanced with a fearsome grimace

(cat. no. 6), was believed to deter the approach of such forces.

The later object is unique in Egyptian art, and its purpose is less certain. The ring held by the god could have been used to present a water lily bud or flower, but the parallel to the earlier object suggests that it may have held an applicator for eye paint. Here the god wears an animal pelt. The square container on his head contains the remnants of a blue substance, perhaps used to affix a headdress of faience feathers (see cat. no. 10), now lost.

BIBLIOGRAPHY

Cat. no. 7: J. D. Cooney, in *Ancient Art: The Norbert Schimmel Collection*, ed. O. W. Muscarella (Mainz: Von Zabern, 1974), no. 211; J. Settgast, ed., *Von Troja bis Amarna: The Norbert Schimmel Collection, New York* (Mainz: Von Zabern, 1978), no. 241; J. F. Romano, "The Bes-Image in Pharaonic Egypt" (PhD diss., New York University, 1989), p. 182; C. H. Roehrig, "Cosmetic Container in the Form of a Bes-Image Holding the Cap of a Kohl Tube," in "Ancient Art: Gifts from the Norbert Schimmel Collection," *BMMA* 49, no. 4 (Spring 1992), pp. 33–34; D. C. Patch, in *Gifts of the Nile: Ancient Egyptian Faience*, ed. F. Friedman, exh. cat. (Providence: Rhode Island School of Design, Museum of Art, 1998), pp. 108, 210.

8. FISH-SHAPED PALETTE

Naqada II, ca. 3650–3300 B.C.
Hierakonpolis (MMA Excavations, 1934–35)
Greywacke
10.3 x 15.3 x 0.4 cm (4 x 6 x ³⁄₁₆ in.)
Rogers Fund, 1935 (35.7.3)

The earliest Predynastic graves contain flat pieces of soft gray stone carved into geometric or animal shapes. This one depicts the fish *Tilapia nilotica* (*bulṭi* in modern Egyptian Arabic). In pharaonic funerary ritual, the transition of the deceased from this life into the hereafter

needed magical assistance, and this species was considered a potent symbol of rebirth. This is one of the most common shapes of Predynastic palettes, so it is likely that the species already possessed significant religious meaning in the Predynastic Period.

The flat sides of the palette served as grinding platforms on which minerals were crushed into powder for use as an eyeliner. The practice of applying an outline of minerals to the eyes, so well known in pharaonic Egypt, was an old tradition. Judging from finds in burials, it would seem that malachite, a green mineral, was the most commonly used eye paint during the Predynastic Period. By the end of Naqada II, small chunks of lead ore (galena) are found in burials alongside malachite and next to the palettes. Eventually black became the preferred color for outlining the eyes; green was largely out of fashion by the end of the Old Kingdom, but it was still used for medicinal purposes.[1]   DCP

NOTE

1. J. F. Nunn, *Ancient Egyptian Medicine* (Norman: University of Oklahoma Press, 1996), pp. 196–97.

BIBLIOGRAPHY

Hayes, *Scepter* I, p. 24.

9. MUMMY BOARD OF INEFERTI

Dynasty 19, reign of Seti I, ca. 1280 B.C.
Thebes, tomb of Sennedjem
Wood, gesso, and paint
182.5 x 44 x 15 cm (71⅞ x 17⁵⁄₁₆ x 5¹⁵⁄₁₆ in.)
Funds from various donors, 1886 (86.1.5C)

Ineferti was the wife of Sennedjem, an artisan of the royal necropolis in Thebes under Seti I (Dynasty 19, ruled ca. 1294–1279 B.C.). This board lay over her

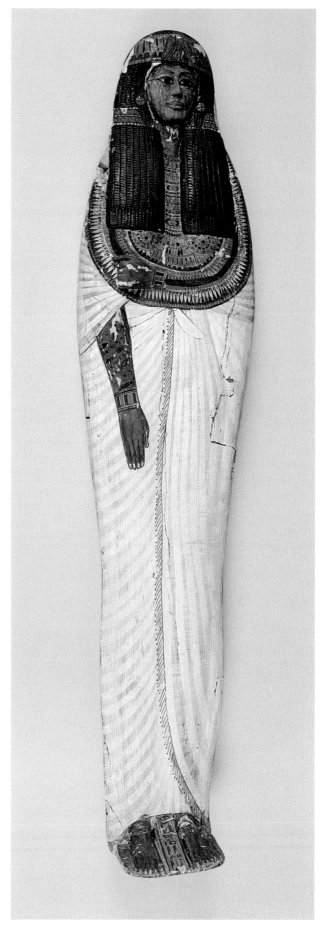

cat. no. 9 (detail of feet)

BIBLIOGRAPHY

E. Toda, "La découverte et l'inventaire du tombeau de Sen-nezem," *Annales du Service des Antiquités de l'Égypte* 20 (1920), pp. 151–55; Hayes, *Scepter* II, p. 415, fig. 264; H. Schneider, *Shabtis: An Introduction to the History of Ancient Egyptian Funerary Statuettes with a Catalogue of the Collection of Shabtis in the National Museum of Antiquities at Leiden* (Leiden: Rijksmuseum van Oudheden, 1977), vol. 1, p. 248; M. Bierbrier, *The Tomb-Builders of the Pharaohs* (London: British Museum, 1982), p. 61, pl. 42; A. Niwinski, *21st Dynasty Coffins from Thebes: Chronological and Typological Studies*, Theben 5 (Mainz: Von Zabern, 1988), p. 159 no. 303; A. Mahmoud, "Ii-neferti, a Poor Woman," *Mitteilungen des Deutschen Archäologischen Instituts, Abteilung Kairo* 55 (1999), pp. 315–23, pl. 50.

10. BES AMULET

Saite–Late Period, ca. 600–400 B.C.
Provenance unknown
Faience
7.2 x 4.6 x 2.3 cm (2 ¹³⁄₁₆ x 1 ¹³⁄₁₆ x ¹⁵⁄₁₆ in.)
Purchase, Edward S. Harkness Gift, 1926 (26.7.1040)

mummy in her coffin, which was buried in her husband's tomb above the workmen's village of Deir el-Medina. It shows her as she appeared during life, wearing a long wig, an elaborate necklace, and a gown of white linen.

Around Ineferti's eyes can be seen black lines representing eye paint. In this case, however, the eyeliner was evidently ineffective as a means of preventing disease; a stela she dedicated to the moon and sun indicates that Ineferti was blind. The text inscribed on the stela beseeches the gods to cure her of this ailment, which she attributes to the malevolent words of some women:

> *Giving praise to the Moon—Thoth, the good god who hears prayers—and kissing the ground to Sunlight, the great god. Be merciful, for you have made me see darkness by day on account of those women's words. May you be merciful to me and let me see your mercy. By the housemistress, Ineferti, justified.*[1]

The slightly off-center and unfocused cast to the eyes on this mummy board suggests the artist's attempt to depict Ineferti's infirmity. On the bottom of the mummy board's feet (ill.) are images of two of Ineferti's daughters weeping for their mother. One of them says, "Don't leave!"

NOTE
1. J. Černý, *Egyptian Stelae in the Bankes Collection* (Oxford: Griffith Institute, 1958), no. 6.

Amulets are the most common of all Egyptian antiquities. Usually made of faience or stone and ranging in size from one to several centimeters in height, they were meant to be worn as protection from malevolent forces and other dangers. Most often, therefore, they represent Egyptian gods or the animals associated with those

gods. This is one of the largest and finest examples. Made in the image of Bes, the amulet depicts in exquisite detail the god's grimacing face, leonine ears and mane, and plumed headdress (see cat. nos. 6, 7). Since Bes was most often invoked for the protection of women and infants, the amulet may have been intended to be worn by a pregnant woman or a young child.

11. BES PLAQUE

Ptolemaic–Early Roman Period, ca. 300 B.C.–1st century A.D.
Provenance unknown
Limestone and paint
38.7 x 17.7 x 5 cm (15 ¼ x 7 x 2 in.)
Rogers Fund, 1922 (22.2.23)

This is one of the more evocative representations of Bes's role as protector. The god is shown grasping a serpent, demonstrating his control over the inimical elements of the ancient Egyptian world, and brandishing a sword, warding off danger from unseen and malevolent forces. The finer details of the god's image, such as the plumes of his headdress (see cat. no. 10), were rendered in paint.

Apart from its clearly defensive function, the exact use of the plaque is unknown. It could have been intended to guard a house or was perhaps displayed outside the bedroom of a mother or child.

12. BES WITH WORSHIPER

Late Period, ca. 500–350 B.C.
Provenance unknown
Bronze
13.2 x 5.5 x 14.5 cm (5 3⁄16 x 2 3⁄16 x 5 11⁄16 in.)
Gift of Darius Ogden Mills, 1904 (04.2.403)

In addition to his role as protector of women, infants, and the home, Bes was also associated with music, perhaps because of the songs mothers have always sung to their children. This aspect of the god is represented here by the lyre he holds.

The god is shown standing on a platform with a ramp, of a type modeled on altars found in the remains of ancient Egyptian houses. In front of him, at a smaller scale, kneels a man in the posture of worship. This figure probably represents the unknown patron for whom the piece was made. His head is shaved, like that of a priest, but this may reflect merely the manner in which the Egyptians felt the gods were to be approached rather than the man's office. Undoubtedly intended as a votive offering, the piece could have been commissioned by its patron to invoke the god's protection of his home and family.

BIBLIOGRAPHY

G. Roeder, *Ägyptische Bronzenfiguren,* Mitteilungen aus der ägyptischen Sammlung 6 (Berlin: Staatliche Museen zu Berlin, 1956), pp. 99§140c, 305§379a, 505§679a, fig. 779.

13. SCARAB

Dynasty 12, reign of Amenemhat III, ca. 1859–1813 B.C.
Probably from Dahshur
Faience
1.6 x 1.1 x 0.7 cm (5⁄8 x 7⁄16 x 5⁄16 in.)
Rogers Fund, 1926 (26.2.1)

In the Egyptian hieroglyphic script, the image of the scarab beetle (*ḫprr*) was used to write the concept "come into being" (*ḫpr*). Worn as an amulet, scarabs represented both the rising sun and the hope of all Egyptians for continued existence in this life and the next. This tiny example of the genre is unusual in its detailed carving. The back is adorned near the head with a cartouche encircling the throne name of Amenemhat III, Nimaatre ("He to Whom the Sun's World-Order Belongs"); below is an image of Bes flanked by two standing hippopotami, each with a crocodile on its back. The scarab's base is engraved with a scene of the pharaoh standing in a skiff and lassoing a hippopotamus in the marshes.

Today crocodiles and hippopotami have retreated to the upper reaches of the Nile in the Sudan and farther south, but during pharaonic times they were two of the most dangerous animals in Egypt. The scene on the scarab's base represents the pharaoh's role in making the country safe for its inhabitants. By their very nature, however, crocodiles and hippopotami were also thought to be as threatening to inimical forces as to the Egyptians themselves, and for this reason they are displayed with Bes on the scarab's back as guardians of its wearer.

Although the scarab was not found in an archaeological context, it most likely came from a royal tomb in the

cat. no. 13 (back)

cat. no. 13 (base)

14. HAIRPIN

Dynasty 12, ca. 1900–1800 B.C.
Provenance unknown
Bone
7 x 1 x 1.1 cm (2¾ x ⅜ x ⁷⁄₁₆ in.)
Rogers Fund, 1907 (07.228.165)

This small pin was used to secure a woman's lock of hair while it was being dressed and was also perhaps part of her finished coiffure (fig. 1). As on the scarab (cat. no. 13), the image of a hippopotamus with a crocodile on its back served to protect the hairpin's owner from unseen forces hostile to her wellbeing. The finely carved details suggest the pin belonged to a woman of high status.

BIBLIOGRAPHY
Hayes, *Scepter* II, p. 38.

dynastic cemetery of Dahshur. The pharaoh's name and image indicate that the scarab was made for a member of the royal family—probably a queen or princess, since Bes and hippopotami usually served as guardians of women. Circumstantial evidence suggests that it belonged to a princess named Ita, who was buried at Dahshur near the pyramid of Amenemhat II (Dynasty 12, ruled ca. 1919–1885 B.C.).

BIBLIOGRAPHY
Hayes, *Scepter* I, p. 239.

Fig. 1. Woman with hairpin. Relief fragment from the tomb of Queen Neferu, Dynasty 11, ca. 2010 B.C. Limestone and paint. The Metropolitan Museum of Art, New York; Rogers Fund, 1926 (26.3.353ww)

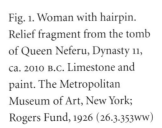

BIBLIOGRAPHY

D. C. Patch, "A Magical Jar", in C. H. Roerhig, ed., *Daughter of Re: Hatshepsut, King of Egypt* (New York: Metropolitan Museum of Art, 2005), in press.

16. HORUS-EYE AMULETS

Saite–Ptolemaic Period, ca. 600–200 B.C.
Provenance unknown
Gold
A. 3.2 x 3.6 x 0.4 cm (1¼ x 1⁷⁄₁₆ x ³⁄₁₆ in.)
B. 3.2 x 4 x 0.4 cm (1¼ x 1⁹⁄₁₆ x ³⁄₁₆ in.)
Rogers Fund, 1923 (23.2.67, 23.2.68)

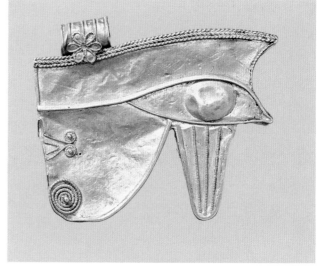

cat. no. 16A

15. MAGICAL CONTAINER

Second Intermediate Period–Dynasty 18, ca. 1700–1500 B.C.
Provenance unknown
Glazed steatite
6.5 x 3.6 x 4 cm (2⁹⁄₁₆ x 1⁷⁄₁₆ x 1⁹⁄₁₆ in.)
Gift of G. Macculloch Miller, 1943 (43.8)

The image of the hippopotamus as a protector of women was itself usually female. During the Middle Kingdom the animal in this role was invoked as the goddess Ipi, but in later periods more often as Taweret ("The Great One"). In this small object the female nature of the hippopotamus is conveyed by the stylized human breasts. The purpose of the cylindrical cavity in its body is uncertain. Whatever it was intended to hold—perhaps a strip of papyrus with magical texts—was meant to be secured by the vessel's lid, which has holes for securing it to the body. The bottom of the base is inscribed with a scroll design like those found on seals. The container's imagery indicates that it was intended for a woman, probably an expectant mother.

JPA and DCP

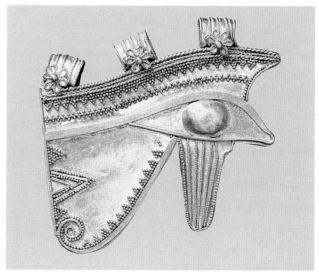

cat. no. 16B

The symbolism of these two amulets was one of the most pervasive and powerful in ancient Egypt. Combining a human eye with the stylized markings of a falcon's, it represents the eye of the god Horus, who is usually depicted as having a human body but the head of a falcon. Horus was one form of the sun god, and the sun itself was seen as his eye; an early myth explained the sun's daily setting and rising as Horus's temporary loss and ultimate recovery of his eye. The restored eye was thus known as the "sound one" and became a symbol of both recovery and prevention from harm.

These two amulets were once part of a necklace. When worn, the necklace served its owner as a guarantee of well-being and a guardian against forces that could threaten health.

BIBLIOGRAPHY
C. R. Clark, "Egyptian Granular Jewelry," *BMMA* 23 (1928), pp. 252–53, fig. 6.

BIRTH AND INFANCY

17. FLINT BLADE

Naqada II, ca. 3650–3300 B.C.
Provenance unknown
Flint
L. 15.7 cm (6³⁄₁₆ in.); W. 5.8 cm (2¼ in.); D. 0.8 cm (⁵⁄₁₆ in.)
Rogers Fund, 1916 (16.2.4)

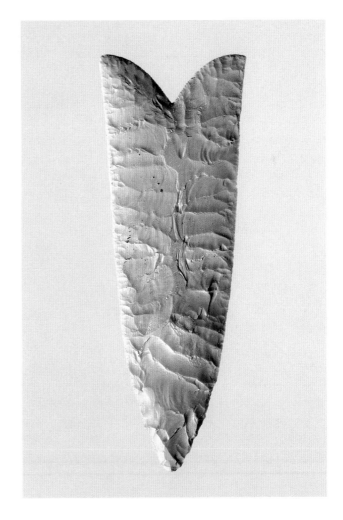

Blades with this distinctive "fish-tail" shape are found in burials throughout the Predynastic Period. They show few, if any, signs of use, an indication that they were either manufactured for purely ceremonial purposes or used briefly during a single ritual event. Although the entire upper portion of the blade has been skillfully edged with miniature sawlike teeth, the cutting surface is actually the V-shaped notch. A few examples have the pointed end hafted in wood. Some blades that have been found were packaged for burial, revealing that they were valued by their owners.[1] One, now in the Metropolitan Museum (20.5), had its cutting edge carefully bound with reeds.

Although the exact purpose or ceremonial role of these blades is unknown, their form suggests an early version of the "flint splitter," an implement used in the "Opening of the Mouth" ceremony during pharaonic funerals (see cat. no. 18).[2] Given this parallel, it is possible that the Predynastic blades were originally designed to cut a newborn's umbilical cord. If so, and if they were thus used for just a single cut at birth and a ritual gesture at the grave, this would certainly account for their excellent condition and careful burial.

DCP

NOTES

1. P. Spencer, "Digging Diary," *Egyptian Archaeology* 25 (2004), pp. 27–28; R. Friedman, personal communication, 2004.
2. A. M. Roth, "The *pss* and the 'Opening of the Mouth' Ceremony: A Ritual of Birth and Rebirth," *Journal of Egyptian Archaeology* 78 (1992), pp. 113–47.

BIBLIOGRAPHY

Hayes, *Scepter* I, p. 19.

18. MODEL OF A MOUTH-OPENING RITUAL SET

Dynasty 5–6, ca. 2400–2200 B.C.
Provenance unknown
Limestone, Egyptian alabaster, and paint
22 x 12 x 3 cm (8 ¹¹⁄₁₆ x 4 ¼ x 1 ³⁄₁₆ in.)
Rogers Fund, 1907 (07.228.117)

Because the ancient Egyptians viewed the afterlife as rebirth, objects associated with human birth became part of their funerary rituals and were often buried with the deceased. This set is a miniature model of objects used in the most important rite of the funeral, the "Opening of the Mouth," which was intended to restore to the spirit the faculties its body had possessed during life.

The shape of the long implement in the center, which the Egyptians called a "flint splitter," derives from that of the flint knives used to cut the umbilical cord of newborns (cat. no. 17). Pressed to the mouth of the deceased's mummy or statue, it symbolically restored the individual's capability of independent existence. The containers on either side are models of the full-scale vessels with which the newly revived spirit was offered milk (a baby's first source of nourishment), salt water (used for cleansing), and fresh water. Buried with the deceased in real or model form after the funeral, these objects were believed to ensure the spirit's continued ability to exist after its daily rebirth at sunrise.

BIBLIOGRAPHY

Hayes, *Scepter* I, p. 118, fig. 70; B. Brier, *Ancient Egyptian Magic* (New York: Morrow, 1980), fig. 65.

19–22. MAGIC WANDS

Dynasty 12, ca. 1900 B.C.
Lisht, North Cemetery, pit 883 (MMA Excavations, 1920–22)
Hippopotamus ivory
4.4 x 34 x 0.3 cm (1 ¾ x 13 ⅜ x ⅛ in.)
Rogers Fund and Edward S. Harkness Gift, 1922 (22.1.103)

Dynasty 12, ca. 1900 B.C.
Lisht, South Cemetery, outer court area, shaft 5004
(MMA Excavations, 1907–8)
Hippopotamus ivory
16 x 33.5 x 0.6 cm (6 ⁵⁄₁₆ x 13 ³⁄₁₆ x ¼ in.)
Rogers Fund, 1908 (08.200.19)

Dynasty 12, ca. 1900 B.C.
Lisht, North Cemetery, tomb 475 (MMA Excavations, 1913–14)
Hippopotamus ivory
4.4 x 26.8 x 0.3 cm (1 ¾ x 10 ⁹⁄₁₆ x ⅛ in.)
Rogers Fund, 1915 (15.3.197)

Dynasty 12–13, ca. 1900–1700 B.C.
Provenance unknown
Hippopotamus ivory
12.5 x 33 x 3.6 cm (4 ¹⁵⁄₁₆ x 13 x 1 ⁷⁄₁₆ in.)
Theodore M. Davis Collection, Bequest of Theodore M. Davis, 1915 (30.8.218)

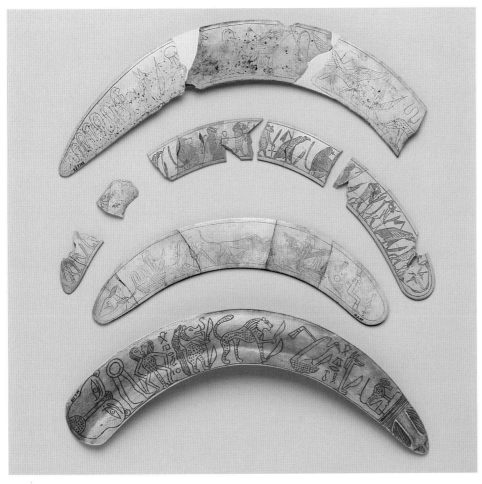

cat. nos. 19–22 (top to bottom)

Among the most evocative of all ancient Egyptian amuletic devices, wands were a common feature in burials of the late Middle Kingdom (ca. 1900–1700 B.C.). Some show signs of wear on one tip (cat. no. 20), suggesting that they were used over a period of time before being placed in the tomb. These examples are decorated on one side with the figures of protective deities, including Bes (cat. no. 22) and a hippopotamus and crocodile (cat. nos. 20–22). Most of the guardians carry knives to ward off evil spirits, and some are shown dispatching the malevolent dead (cat. no. 21).

The purpose of these objects is revealed by an inscription carved on the back of catalogue number 20: "Recitation by the many protectors: We have come that we may extend our protection around the healthy child Minhotep, alive, sound, and healthy, born of the noblewoman Sitsobek, alive, sound, and healthy." Two (cat. nos. 21, 22) are also inscribed on the front with the words "protection by day" and "protection by night." The texts indicate that the wands were used to defend infants against malign forces, perhaps by scratching a circle in the earth around the area where they slept. Many of the figures are of deities associated with the sun's passage through the netherworld at night, including baboons, lions, jackal-headed gods, serpents, and images of fire. These were evidently invoked to protect the infant at night, as they did the sun. Figures of a vulture

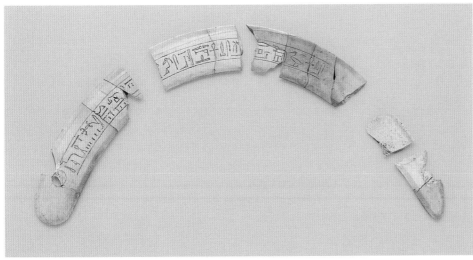

cat. no. 20 (back)

Fig. 2. Magic wand shown as found, wrapped in linen. Egyptian Museum, Cairo. Photograph courtesy Deutsches Archäologisches Institut, Cairo

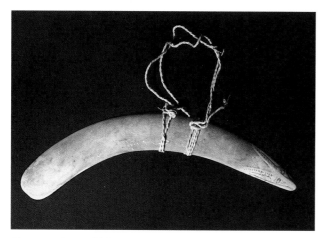

Fig. 3. Magic wand (fig. 2) unwrapped, with original cord. Egyptian Museum, Cairo. Photograph courtesy Deutsches Archäologisches Institut, Cairo

recall the hieroglyph with which the word "mother" was written, perhaps as a guarantee of rebirth at dawn. Having provided defense against illness during life, after death the wands were placed in the tomb to ensure the continued protection of the deceased's spirit in its eternal afterlife. Figures 2 and 3 show one such wand as it was found (wrapped in linen) and with its attached cord, which was used to carry or manipulate the wand.

BIBLIOGRAPHY
Cat. nos. 19, 21: Hayes, *Scepter* I, pp. 248–49, fig. 159; B. Brier, *Ancient Egyptian Magic* (New York: Morrow, 1980), p. 49, fig. 9. *Cat. no. 20:* H. Altenmüller, "Ein Zaubermesse des Mittleren

Reiches," *Studien zur altägyptischen Kultur* 13 (1986), pp. 22–24; D. Arnold, *The South Cemeteries of Lisht,* vol. 3, *The Pyramid Complex of Senwosret I,* Publications of The Metropolitan Museum of Art Egyptian Expedition 25 (New York: MMA, 1992), pp. 47, 69–70, pls. 82–84a; M. Hill, in *The American Discovery of Ancient Egypt,* ed. N. Thomas, exh. cat. (Los Angeles: Los Angeles County Museum of Art, 1995), p. 155. *Cat. no 21:* A. C. Mace, "Excavations at the North Pyramid of Lisht," *BMMA* 9 (1914), pp. 218, 220, fig. 11; H. G. Fischer, "Some Iconographic and Literary Comparisons," in *Fragen an die altägyptische Literatur: Studien zum Gedenken an Eberhard Otto,* ed. J. Assmann et al. (Wiesbaden: Reichert, 1977), p. 166, fig. 1. *Cat. nos. 21, 22:* H. E. Winlock, "The Egyptian Expedition, 1930–1931," *BMMA* 27 (March 1932), part 2, pp. 36–37; G. Steindorff, "The Magical Knives of Ancient Egypt," *Journal of the Walters Art Gallery* 9 (1946), p. 106n41, fig. 4. *Cat. no. 22:* H. G. Fischer, *Ancient Egyptian Representations of Turtles,* The Metropolitan Museum of Art Papers 13 (New York: MMA, 1968), p.11n24; P. Dorman, in "Egyptian Art," ed. C. Lilyquist, *BMMA* 41, no. 3 (Winter 1983–84), p. 20, no. 18.

23. BABY'S FEEDING CUP

Dynasty 12, ca. 1900–1800 B.C.
Lisht, North Cemetery (MMA Excavations, 1906–7)
Faience
H. 3.5 cm (1⅜ in.); W. 8 cm (3⅛ in.)
Rogers Fund, 1944 (44.4.4)

Liquids were fed to an infant through the small hole in the spout of this little vessel. The figures that march around the exterior are similar to those found on magic wands of the same period (see cat. nos. 19–22). Here they include, on the vessel's right side, a turtle, a lion with a serpent over its back, a fantastic beast with a knife over its back, and a standing lion grasping a serpent; the same ones appear on the left side, except that instead of a standing lion there is a standing hippopotamus with a crocodile holding a knife and the hieroglyph for "protection." On the back (opposite the spout) is a standing figure flanked by two images of Bes holding serpents. The presence of these guardian deities on the cup ensured that the contents would be healthy for the infant who drank from it.

BIBLIOGRAPHY
Hayes, *Scepter* I, p. 247; H. G. Fischer, "Egyptian Turtles," *BMMA* 24 (1965–66), p. 197, fig. 9; H. G. Fischer, *Ancient Egyptian Representations of Turtles,* The Metropolitan Museum of Art

Papers 13 (New York: MMA, 1968), pp. 16, 33, no. 95, pl. 20; P. Charvát, "The Bes Jug: Its Origin and Development in Egypt," *Zeitschrift für ägyptische Sprache und Altertumskunde* 107 (1980), p. 48; J. F. Romano, "The Bes-Image in Pharaonic Egypt" (PhD diss., New York University, 1989), n. 58; D. C. Patch, in *Gifts of the Nile: Ancient Egyptian Faience*, ed. F. Friedman, exh. cat. (Providence: Rhode Island School of Design, Museum of Art, 1998), pp. 105, 207.

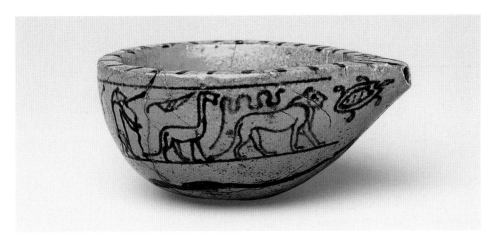

24. GUARDIAN FIGURE

Dynasty 12–13, ca. 1900–1700 B.C.
Lisht, North Cemetery (MMA Excavations, 1913–14)
Wood
10.7 x 4 x 2 cm (4¼ x 1⁹⁄₁₆ x ¾ in.)
Rogers Fund, 1915 (15.3.1088)

Despite its ruined state, this little statue is a plaintive witness to the role of magic in ancient Egyptian health. It was found in the Middle Kingdom cemetery at Lisht, where it had been placed either in a grave or as an offering above a tomb. The figure's lion mane and ears are those of the god Bes, but its body is quite unlike the round, dwarfish torso with which the god is regularly depicted (see cat. nos. 6, 7, 11, 12), suggesting that it represents the god's much rarer female counterpart, Beset. Like Bes, this goddess was a guardian of mothers during and after childbirth and of their infants. In the cemetery, Beset's presence would have offered the same protection to the deceased in their daily rebirth to new life as a spirit.

25. TAWERET

Ptolemaic Period, ca. 300–30 B.C.
Qena region
Glass
11 x 3.3 x 4.6 cm (4 5⁄16 x 1 5⁄16 x 1 13⁄16 in.)
Purchase, Edward S. Harkness Gift, 1926 (26.7.1193)

This beautifully crafted statue represents the classic form of the hippopotamus goddess Taweret, guardian of women, particularly in pregnancy and childbirth. It could have been given as a gift to a pregnant women or presented in a temple to invoke Taweret's aid in a successful birth. The figure's pendant breasts are those of a human female, and her protruding belly is that of a pregnant woman. In front of her she holds the hieroglyphic symbol for "protection," an explicit statement of her role in Egyptian life. The tang on her head may have once secured a headdress (see cat. no. 26).

BIBLIOGRAPHY
J. D. Cooney, "Glass Sculpture in Ancient Egypt," *Journal of Glass Studies* 2 (1960), pp. 29–30, fig. 22.

26. STELA OF TAWERET AND MUT

Dynasty 18–19, ca. 1400–1200 B.C.
Thebes, Deir el-Medina
Limestone and paint
17.7 x 14.3 x 4 cm (7 x 5 5⁄8 x 1 9⁄16 in.)
Dodge Fund, 1947 (47.105.4)

This small stela depicts Taweret together with Mut, another goddess associated with women. Although the two deities face each other, in the conventions of Egyptian art they are meant to be seen as standing side by side, facing the viewer. Between them is a jar of water on a stand (see cat. no. 2) and a water lily (see cat. nos. 43–46).

Taweret appears on the left, identified by the inscription in front of her as "Taweret, mistress of the sky." On her head she wears a sun disk and cow's horns. Although Taweret herself is not usually associated with the sky, this feature, and her epithet, are probably borrowed from Hathor, the goddess of femininity and love, indicating that here Taweret represents the female sex itself. In keeping with her usual role as a protective force for women during and after childbirth, her protruding belly suggests pregnancy. She is also shown emerging from an acacia tree. The seedpods of the acacia, which have astringent and antibacterial properties, were used to treat uterine complaints and could be applied after childbirth to prevent infection.

The image on the right is identified by its inscription as "Mut the great, mistress of Isheru." This goddess was the wife of Amun and embodied the principle of motherhood; her name means "mother." She is represented here by a human head atop a chest, which may be a symbolic representation of the womb. Her headdress, like Taweret's, reflects an association with Hathor.

The stela was commissioned by a man whose name and partially preserved title are inscribed at bottom: "[. . .] of [the house of] Amun, Khonsu." His name is the same as that of the god who was the son of Amun and Mut. The stela's imagery suggests that it was intended as a votive offering by its donor, who was seeking, probably on behalf of his wife, the intercession of Taweret and Mut for a successful pregnancy and childbirth.

BIBLIOGRAPHY

N. E. Scott, "Egyptian Accessions," *BMMA* 6 (1947–48), p. 63; L. Keimer, review of *The Treasure of Three Egyptian Princesses*, by H. E. Winlock, *Bibliotheca Orientalis* 6 (1949), p. 138, pl. 4, fig. 3; Hayes, *Scepter* II, p. 385, fig. 242; R. M. Freed, *A Divine Tour of Ancient Egypt*, exh. cat. (Memphis, Tenn.: Memphis State University, 1983), p. 73; L. S. Russo, "L'uso domestico della magia: alcune stele apotropaiche," in *La magia in Egitto ai tempi dei faraoni*, ed. A. Roccati and A. Siliotti (Milan: Rassegna Internazionale di Cinematografia Archeologica, Arte e Natura Libri, 1987), pp. 215–16, fig. 9; A. P. Kozloff, in *Egypt's Dazzling Sun: Amenhotep III and His World*, ed. A. P. Kozloff and B. Bryan, exh. cat. (Cleveland: Cleveland Museum of Art, 1992), p. 403, fig. 105a; A. K. Capel, in *Mistress of the House, Mistress of Heaven: Women in Ancient Egypt*, exh. cat. (Cincinnati: Cincinnati Art Museum, 1996), p. 130.

27–28. ANTHROPOID JARS

Dynasty 18, ca. 1400 B.C.
Saqqara
Pottery and paint
15.4 x 7 x 6.5 cm (6 1/16 x 2 3/4 x 2 9/16 in.)
Rogers Fund, 1926 (26.2.30)

Dynasty 18, ca. 1400 B.C.
Provenance unknown
Pottery and paint
15.3 x 8 x 8 cm (6 x 3 1/8 x 3 1/8 in.)
Gift of Dr. and Mrs. Thomas H. Foulds, 1925 (25.7.42)

The ancient Egyptians considered the act of nursing and breast milk important both for the well-being of the living child and in the process of rebirth (see cat.

no. 30). A reliable supply of breast milk, whether from the mother herself or from a wet nurse, was deemed essential, and it is possible that these jars were made to hold the surplus. Perhaps because of its life-sustaining qualities, breast milk was also included in medical prescriptions for head colds, burns, rashes, and fever in adults as well as infants.

The capacity of these jars, about one-tenth of a liter, has been calculated to be approximately the amount of milk that a mother's breast can produce at one feeding.[1] The heads on them (and in catalogue number 28 the overall form) reflect the human origin of their contents; in one example of the genre, the woman is even depicted milking her breast into a cup.[2] The horn-shaped container held by the woman in catalogue number 28, however, probably represents an ointment dispenser, since rubbing certain ointments on the back of a nursing mother was believed to stimulate milk production.

Female-figure jars like these were produced only for a short time—from the middle of the reign of Thutmose III to that of Amenhotep III (ca. 1450–1350 B.C.)—and are all probably products of a single workshop.[3]

SJA

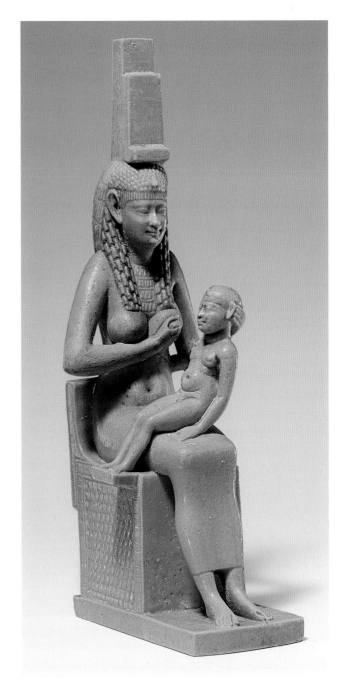

NOTES
1. E. Brunner-Traut, "Das Muttermilchkrüglein: Ammen mit Stillumhang und Mondamulett," *Die Welt des Orients* 5 (1970), pp. 145–64; R. M. and J. J. Janssen, *Growing up in Ancient Egypt* (London: Rubicon Press, 1990), p. 19.
2. G. Robins, *Women in Ancient Egypt* (Cambridge, Mass.: Harvard University Press, 1993), p. 81.
3. J. Bourriau, "Pottery Figure Vases of the New Kingdom," *Cahiers de la céramique égyptienne* 1 (1987), pp. 81–96.

BIBLIOGRAPHY
Hayes, *Scepter* II, p. 195, fig. 110.

29. ISIS NURSING HORUS

Ptolemaic Period, ca. 300–30 B.C.
Provenance unknown
Faience
17 x 5 x 6.9 cm (6 11/16 x 2 x 2 ¾ in.)
Purchase, Joseph Pulitzer Bequest, 1955 (55.121.5)

Mut appears as a goddess of motherhood during and after the New Kingdom (see cat. no. 26), but throughout ancient Egyptian history the most important goddess with that role was Isis. Wife of Osiris and mother of their son, Horus, Isis was the link between the gods who represented the formation of the world and the inhabitants of that world. She was worshiped as the mother of all living beings, human and divine, and the relationship between her and Horus was seen as the model for motherhood.

In this statue Isis is shown preparing to nurse the infant Horus. She is seated on a throne and wears on her head the hieroglyph for "seat," with which her name is spelled. The cult of Isis became especially important in the Ptolemaic Period. The statue was probably intended as a votive offering to her, perhaps from someone seeking the goddess's intercession for a mother and her child.

BIBLIOGRAPHY
N. E. Scott, "Recent Additions to the Egyptian Collection," *BMMA* 15 (November 1956), p. 87.

30. NURSING WOMAN

Dynasty 5–6, ca. 2400–2200 B.C.
Giza
Limestone and paint
11 x 6 x 7 cm (4⁵⁄₁₆ x 2³⁄₈ x 2¾ in.)
Purchase, Edward S. Harkness Gift, 1926 (26.7.1405)

Where the statue of Isis and Horus (cat. no. 29) honors the act of nursing in the abstract, this miniature group reflects its importance in the world of human beings. Like Isis, the woman here is preparing to nurse the baby held on her knee; a second, older child reaches for the other breast from behind and under the woman's arm. This piece belongs to a genre traditionally known as "servant statues": images of men and women engaged in everyday tasks that were immured in tombs from the Fourth to Sixth Dynasty (ca. 2500–2200 B.C.). Once thought to represent servants working on behalf of the tomb owner, they have recently been identified as images of the tomb owner himself and of members of his family.[1]

The Egyptians saw nursing as an essential component of the afterlife, which they understood as a process of daily rebirth. The funerary liturgy known as the Pyramid Texts, contemporary with this statue, reflect this view in a dialogue between the deceased and his spiritual mother:

> *"My mother," I say, "give me your breast that I may suck from it."*
> *"My son," she says, "receive my breast and suck from it," she says, "that you may live," she says, "for you are a small child" (PT 470).*

For the owner of the tomb in which it was placed, this little group served as an eternal guarantee of access to the life-giving nourishment it depicts.

NOTE
1. A. M. Roth, "The Meaning of Menial Labor: 'Servant Statues' in Old Kingdom Serdabs," *JARCE* 39 (2002), pp. 103–21.

BIBLIOGRAPHY
J. H. Breasted Jr., *Egyptian Servant Statues,* Bollingen Series 13 (Washington, D.C.: Pantheon, 1948), p. 97; Hayes, *Scepter* I, p. 113; W. S. Smith, *A History of Egyptian Scuplture and Painting in the Old Kingdom* (1946; New York: Hacker, 1978), pp. 58, 71, 101, pl. 27.

31. COFFIN AND MUMMY OF NESIAMUN

Dynasty 25, ca. 700 B.C.
Thebes, Deir el-Bahri
Wood and paint; human remains, linen, and resin
196.5 x 54 x 43 cm (77⅜ x 21¼ x 16¹⁵⁄₁₆ in.)
Rogers Fund, 1926 (26.3.11)

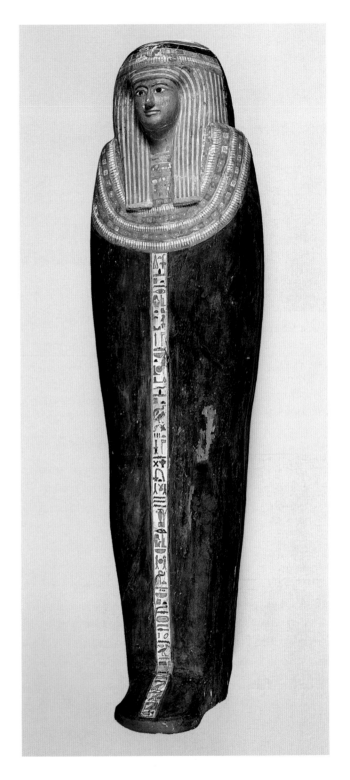

This anthropoid coffin, discovered by the Metropolitan Museum during its 1922–23 season of excavation in Thebes, was buried in a Middle Kingdom tomb in an area known as the "Priests' Cemetery," adjacent to the mortuary temple complex of Mentuhotep II (Dynasty 11, ruled ca. 2051–2000 B.C.). The inscription down the center of the lid identifies its owner:

> *A royal offering of Osiris, foremost of the west, the great god, lord of Abydos, giving an offering of food, incense on the fire, linen and clothing, and cool water (to) the Osiris, lord of continuity, ruler of eternity, and first lord, Nesiamun, justified, son of Bakenamun, justified, whose mother is Tahathor, justified.*

Nesiamun's name and that of his father both honor Amun, the chief god of Thebes; judging from his coffin's provenance and style, it is probable that Nesiamun lived in that city during the Twenty-fifth Dynasty.

Although his mummy has never been unwrapped, a recent CAT (computer-assisted tomography) scan revealed that Nesiamun was 166 cm (5 ft. 5⅜ in.) tall and sustained several serious injuries before death. Figure 4 shows gross disruption of his ribs, a fracture of the right humerus, and a linear skull fracture. The fracture site in the humerus is surrounded by healing bone (callus), indicating that Nesiamun lived for several weeks after his injuries. Figure 5 shows the fracture of his pelvis and the odd placement by the embalmers of extraneous bones within his abdominal cavity, along with two rod-like structures on either side of his spine; a third rod occupies the center of his spinal column, apparently displacing the nerves and spinal cord.

Our examination of the CAT images, in consultation with the chief medical examiner of New York City, concluded that Nesiamun's trauma was probably the result of a vehicular accident. The impact of a chariot or horse could have caused the broken pelvis, with the other frac-tures secondary to the fall. Although the inscription on Nesiamun's coffin gives no clue as to his occupation, it is also possible that he was a military casualty or that he

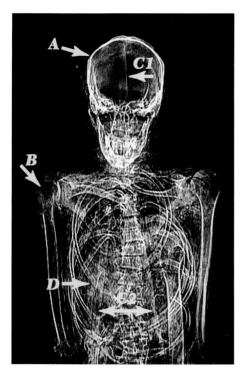

Fig. 4. CAT scan of the mummy of Nesiamun.
A. Linear fracture on right side of skull.
B. Fracture site in right humerus, with callus.
C. Papyrus rods, vertically traversing the head
(1) and paraspinal (2). D. Packet probably
containing mummified internal organs.

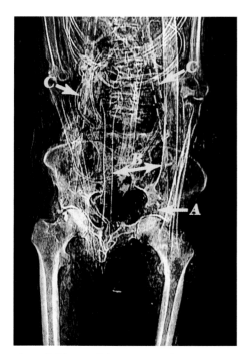

Fig. 5. CAT scan of the mummy of Nesiamun.
A. Fractured pelvis with some distortion from
curvature of the spine. B. Extraneous bones
loose in the abdomen. C. Paraspinal rods
extending to the end of the torso.

was injured while working on a building project. The extraneous bones and rods were placed by the embalmers probably in order to stabilize Nesiamun's badly damaged body. The New York Botanical Garden has identified the rods as either cyperus papyrus or the center rib of a date palm frond.

DTM

BIBLIOGRAPHY
D. T. Mininberg, "A 25th-Dynasty Vehicular Accident," *KMT* 11, no. 3 (Fall 2000), pp. 60–66.

32. MUMMY PORTRAIT

Roman Period, ca. A.D. 160
Fayum
Encaustic paint on wood
H. 35 cm (13¾ in.); W. 17.2 cm (6¾ in.)
Rogers Fund, 1909 (09.181.4)

This portait was executed in encaustic, a complex technique in which paint was mixed with beeswax, resin,

egg, or linseed oil. The resulting medium could be applied using a heated implement or softened with heat and applied by brush. Such portraits, which in the Roman Period were bound in place over the face of a mummy, depict the deceased as he or she looked during life and are among the earliest preserved examples of true portrait painting.

The young man portrayed here has a right eye smaller than the left. The artist's depiction suggests that the cause of this microphthalmic condition was congenital, as the whole eye is smaller, the corneal diameter is diminished, and there is some facial asymmetry; the right mandible (jawbone) also appears more developed and prominent than the left. A healed, horizontal surgical incision compromising the lower eyelashes is depicted on the lower right eyelid. This surgery might have been performed to improve the vision in that eye or to repair a traumatic lesion, but the latter scenario is less likely given the other abnormalities in the eye.

One ancient Egyptian medical text, known as the Ebers Papyrus, cites more than thirty cases of eye diseases and their treatment. Of these, nine were treated surgically, including growths, infected growths (abscesses), overgrowth of vessels (varix), twisted vessels (hemangioma), and extraction of parasites. Egyptian physicians treated inflammation of the eye (ophthalmia) with drugs, including copper and antimony. They understood the seasonal cycle of these inflammations and their different presentations: corneal infiltrates known as leucomata (white spots) occurred during the inundation (June–September), when the disease was usually incurred; tearing and watering of the eyes from acute inflammation were prevalent in the following months (October–January); and treatment for the late stages of disease was often needed during harvest season (February–May). The multiple containers in some kohl jars (see cat. no. 5) may reflect the need for different therapeutic applications according to the season.

D A and D T M

BIBLIOGRAPHY

A. M. Lythgoe, "Graeco-Egyptian Portraits," *BMMA* 5 (1910), p. 68, fig. 4; H. Drerup, *Die Datierung der Mumienporträts,* Studien zur Geschichte und Kultur des Altertums 19, no. 1 (Paderborn: Schöningh, 1933), pp. 42, 61, pl. 15a; K. Parlasca, *Mumienporträts und verwandte Denkmäler* (Wiesbaden: Steiner, 1966), pp. 42n172, 132, 253; J. E. Berger, *L'oeil et l'éternité: Portraits romains d'Égypte* (Paudex: Fontainemore-Flammarion, 1977), p. 216; K. Parlasca,

Ritratti di mummie, Repertorio d'arte dell'Egitto greco-romano, ser. B, Pittura, vol. 2 (Rome: "L'Erma" di Bretschneider, 1977), p. 85, no. 470, pl. 114.2; E. Doxiadis, *The Mysterious Fayum Portraits: Faces from Ancient Egypt* (London and New York: Thames and Hudson, 1995), pp. 153–54, 219 no. 96; U. Schädler, "Porträt eines jungen Mannes," in *Augenblicke: Mumienporträts und ägyptische Grabkunst aus römischer Zeit,* ed. K. Parlasca and H. Seemann, exh. cat. (Frankfurt: Schirn Kunsthalle, 1999), pp. 342–43; S. Walker: *Ancient Faces: Mummy Portraits from Roman Egypt,* exh. cat. (New York: MMA, 2000), pp. 115–16.

33. BATTLE SCENE

Dynasty 18, reign of Amenhotep II, ca. 1427–1400 B.C.
Thebes, el-Asasif
Sandstone and paint
61 x 115 x 40 cm (24 x 45¼ x 15¾ in.)
Rogers Fund, 1913 (13.180.21)

This block was once part of a large relief showing the pharaoh vanquishing his Syrian enemies. The Metropolitan Museum's Theban Expedition discovered it in 1912–13 in the unfinished mortuary temple of Ramesses IV (Dynasty 20, ruled ca. 1153–1147 B.C.), where it had been used as part of the temple's foundations. (This reuse accounts for the preservation of its vivid paint.) The Syrians are shown falling beneath the horses drawing the pharaoh's chariot; the animals' legs, bellies, and genitalia can be seen at the block's upper right margin. Typically in such scenes the pharaoh is depicted shooting a bow, and here we see three of the enemy struck by his arrows (the carved arrow in the second figure from the right was ignored by the painter). The other Syrians are evidently being trampled by the hooves of the pharaoh's horses.

The battle scene depicted here was one of many fought by pharaohs of the Eighteenth Dynasty to secure Egypt's eastern border after the expulsion of the Asiatic rulers known as Hyksos (see cat. no. 60). Although these wounded are foreigners, their injuries are typical of those sustained in combat by Egyptian soldiers and subsequently treated by Egyptian physicians (see cat. no. 31).

BIBLIOGRAPHY

H. E. Winlock, "Excavations at Thebes in 1912–13, by the Museum's Egyptian Expedition," *BMMA* 9 (1914), pp. 22–23, fig. 12; G. Steindorff, *Egypt,* 2nd ed. (New York: Augustin, 1945), p. 132; W. S. Smith, *The Art and Architecture of Ancient Egypt* (Baltimore:

Penguin, 1958), pl. 160A; Hayes, *Scepter* II, p. 340, fig. 214;
P. Dorman, in "Egyptian Art," ed. C. Lilyquist, *BMMA* 41,
no. 3 (Winter 1983–84), pp. 42–43, no. 42; P. Dorman, in *The
Metropolitan Museum of Art: Egypt and the Ancient Near East*,
ed. P. Dorman et al. (New York: MMA, 1987), pp. 70–71; P. Brand,
in *The American Discovery of Ancient Egypt*, ed. N. Thomas,
exh. cat. (Los Angeles: Los Angeles County Museum of Art, 1995),
pp. 170–71; I. Franco, "Block with Conquered Asians," in *The
Pharaohs*, ed. C. Ziegler (Milan: Bompiani, 2002), p. 424.

34–35. BOW AND ARROWS

Dynasty 18, ca. 1460 B.C.
Thebes, Sheikh Abd el-Qurna
Wood
L. 173 cm (68⅛ in.); W. 7.5 cm (3 in.); Diam. 2.6 cm (1 in.)
Rogers Fund, 1936 (36.3.211)

Dynasty 12, ca. 1900–1800 B.C.
Provenance unknown
Reed, paint, flint, and linen twine
L. 73–76 cm (28¾–30 in.); Diam. 0.5 cm (³⁄₁₆ in.)
Rogers Fund, 1912 (12.183.53)

Although manufactured some four centuries apart, this
bow and six arrows are typical of those used by Egyptian
soldiers in battle at the time the Edwin Smith Papyrus

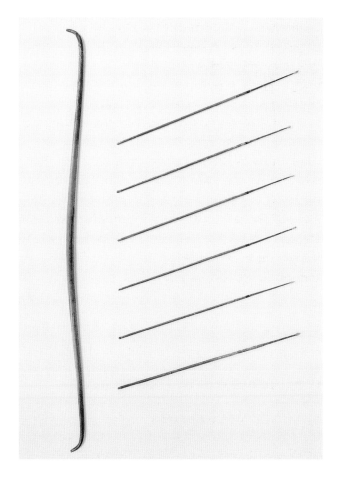

(cat. no. 60) was written. The bow is one of two found (with a different set of arrows) in a cache below the hillside tomb of Senenmut, an official of the pharaoh Hatshepsut (Dynasty 18, ruled ca. 1473–1458 B.C.). It shows no signs of use and was evidently made as part of a burial assemblage. The arrows, made about four hundred years earlier, have flint chips embedded, glued, and tied into their heads; they are of the length that would have been used with longbows like catalogue number 34. The bow itself is powerful enough to drive such arrows, even without arrowheads, through the body of an enemy.

BIBLIOGRAPHY
Cat. no. 34: Hayes, *Scepter* II, p. 211, fig. 125 (36.3.211); *Cat. no. 35*: Hayes, *Scepter* I, p. 280 (12.183.53).

36. BATTLE-AX

Dynasty 18, ca. 1460 B.C.
Thebes, el-Asasif, tomb 729 (east chamber), burial 8
Wood and bronze; modern rawhide
L. 55.5 cm (21⅞ in.) restored; W. 16.5 cm (6½ in.) at blade
Rogers Fund, 1935 (35.3.56)

Axes of this type were used by Egyptian soldiers as well as their enemies in the late Seventeenth Dynasty, the era of the Edwin Smith Papyrus (cat. no. 60), and could easily have caused a number of the injuries described in that document. The mummy of the Seventeenth Dynasty pharaoh Seqenenre (ruled ca. 1556–1552 B.C.),

now in the Egyptian Museum, Cairo, shows that he was killed in battle by this kind of weapon.

The ax was found in the family tomb of an official of the early Eighteenth Dynasty and may have been wielded by its owner in one of the many battle campaigns of Thutmose III (ruled ca. 1479–1425 B.C.). Only the ax head itself and the lower part of the handle are ancient. The weapon has been restored based on more completely preserved examples from the period.

BIBLIOGRAPHY
W. C. Hayes, "The Tomb of Nefer-khēwet and His Family," in "The Egyptian Expedition, 1934–1935," *BMMA* 30 (November 1935), part 2, p. 32, fig. 17; Hayes, *Scepter* II, p. 211, fig. 125.

37–38. MODEL SPEARS, SPEAR CASE, AND SHIELD

Dynasty 12, ca. 1950 B.C.
Asyut
Wood, gesso, and paint
Spears: L. 50.6–52 cm (19¹⁵⁄₁₆–20½ in.)
Case: H. 41.6 cm (16⅜ in.); Diam. 7.8 cm (3¹⁄₁₆ in.)
Shield: H. 71.5 cm (28³⁄₁₆ in.); W. 42.2 cm (16⅝ in.)
Gift of Edward S. Harkness, 1917 (17.9.3–11)

Besides bows and arrows and battle-axes (cat. nos. 34–36), Egyptian soldiers going into combat also carried spears and protected themselves with shields, and these models, made for the burial of a Middle Kingdom official,

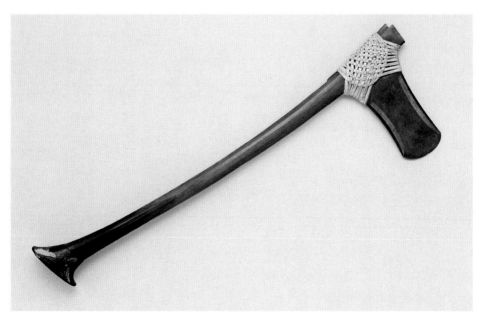

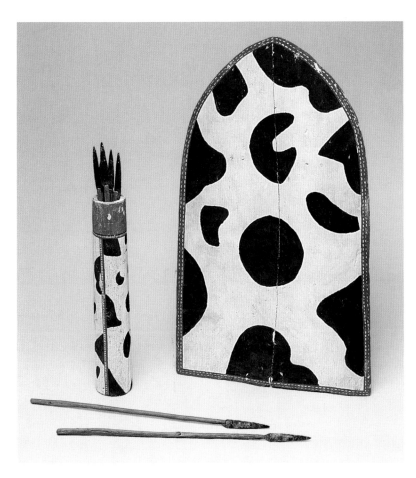

are faithful reproductions of Egyptian military equipment. Real spears, which would have been about the same length, had flint or metal heads and were meant for use in close-quarter combat. Spear cases and shields were made of cowhide. The shields had a wood grip, but otherwise they consisted only of hide, which evidently was stiff and thick enough to repel both arrows and ax blows; their composition also made them light and easily maneuverable. The shield was reinforced at its edges with a strip of rawhide, here indicated in red paint.

BIBLIOGRAPHY

Anon., "The Fiftieth Anniversary Exhibition," *BMMA* 15 (1920), p. 129; Hayes, *Scepter* I, p. 278, fig. 180.

TREATMENT

39. HEART AMULET

Dynasty 19–20, ca. 1200–1100 B.C.
Provenance unknown
Green stone
2.8 x 2 x 1 cm (1⅛ x ¾ x ⅜ in.)
Gift of Helen Miller Gould, 1910 (10.130.1797)

Egyptian physicians usually did not practice internal surgery, and detailed knowledge of the human body's interior was generally limited to embalmers. In fact, the Egyptians were much more familiar with the internal organs of their livestock (cattle, sheep, and goats), since most families slaughtered and prepared their own meat. This is reflected in the hieroglyphic signs for internal organs, which are mostly those of mammals other than humans.

A case in point is this small sculpture of a heart, which is bovine in form. Like others of its kind, it was intended for use as an amulet, most likely on the body of a human mummy. The Egyptians recognized the central role of the heart in the circulatory system, as the explanation in Case 1 of the Edwin Smith Papyrus (cat. no. 60) makes clear, but they also identified the heart rather than the brain as the seat of thought and emotion, a concept that still exists in such expressions as "disheartened" and "broken-hearted." Such amulets were meant to ensure the eternal preservation of the deceased's intellectual and emotional faculties.

40. HONEY-JAR LABEL

Dynasty 18, reign of Amenhotep III, ca. 1390–1352 B.C.
Thebes, Malqatta
Pottery and ink
8.5 x 16 x 3 cm (3⅜ x 6⁵⁄₁₆ x 1¹⁄₁₆ in.)
Rogers Fund, 1917 (17.10.12)

Honey was the most important and sometimes the only sweetener used throughout ancient Egyptian history. Besides its sweetness, honey contains antibacterial agents and acts as an osmotic, drawing moisture from whatever it is applied to. Although Egyptian physicians were unaware of bacteria, they observed the therapeutic and osmotic benefits of honey when it is applied to wounds, and they therefore made honey a central component of their pharmacopoeia. The Edwin Smith Papyrus (cat. no. 60) prescribes it in thirty of forty-eight cases and includes it in two of the prescriptions on the verso.

The honey stored in the jar to which these two sherds belonged was probably meant for use as a sweetener, although it could also have served as a medicament. The sherds were found by the Metropolitan Museum's excavations at Malqatta, site of a Theban palace of Amenhotep III and his family. The ink inscription, written in hieratic (the cursive form of hieroglyphs), indicates that the jar was the "produce of the living Queen's house" and contained "red (i.e., dark) honey." The sign at the beginning (right-hand side) of the second line is that of a bee, with which the word for "honey" was written (see cat. no. 56 for a hieroglyphic example of the same sign). Similar inscriptions from Malqatta indicate that the third line, now mostly lost, contained the name of Amenemhat, the high priest of Heliopolis. The honey was apparently donated to the royal family on his behalf.

41–42. POMEGRANATE JARS

Dynasty 19–20, ca. 1280–1080 B.C.
Provenance unknown
Glass
H. 6.8 cm (2¹¹⁄₁₆ in.); Diam. 5.8 cm (2¼ in.)
Rogers Fund, 1944 (44.4.52)

Dynasty 20, ca. 1180–1080 B.C.
Probably from Abydos, Tell el-Manshiya
Glass
H. 12 cm (4¾ in.); Diam. 7.9 cm (3⅛ in.)
Purchase, Edward S. Harkness Gift, 1926 (26.7.1180)

Pomegranates were introduced into Egypt from western Asia during the New Kingdom (ca. 1550–1295 B.C.) Their juice was prized as a drink, but it can also be used as an astringent to shrink tissues and reduce swelling in wounds. In addition, the root of pomegranate trees is prescribed in medical papyri as a vermifuge against intestinal worms—its active ingredient, pelletrin, is still used for this purpose—and the juice is helpful in treating stomach disorders such as dysentery and diarrhea. These two jars were no

doubt made to hold pomegranate juice, probably for consumption as a drink but possibly for medicinal purposes as well. The latter use is perhaps likelier for the smaller, green jar, which depicts the fruit in its unripened state, when the juice is too sour to drink.

Glassmaking, like pomegranates, arrived in Egypt during the New Kingdom, perhaps also as an import from western Asia. These two vessels were formed around a clay core, which was scraped out after the glass had cooled and hardened. The rims were made by reheating, cutting, and pressing the glass into shape.

J P A and D T M

BIBLIOGRAPHY

Cat. no. 41: Hayes, *Scepter* II, p. 404, fig. 255; B. Schlick-Nolte, *Die Glasgefässe im alten Ägypten,* Münchener Ägyptologische Studien 14 (Berlin: Hessling, 1968), pp. 42, 760 no. 6, pl. 27 no. 42; S. M. Goldstein, in *Egypt's Golden Age: The Art of Living in the New Kingdom, 1558– 1085 B.C.,* exh. cat. (Boston: Museum of Fine Arts, 1982), p. 168; S. J. Allen, "Vase in the Shape of a Pomegranate," in "Ars Vitraria," *BMMA* 59, no. 1 (Summer 2001), p. 14.

43. WATER LILY MODELS

Dynasty 11, ca. 2000 B.C.
Thebes, Deir el-Bahri, pits in the triangular court north of the mortuary temple of Mentuhotep II
Wood, gesso, and paint
A. H. 10 cm (3 ¹⁵⁄₁₆ in.); Diam. 5.5 cm (2 ³⁄₁₆ in.)
B. H. 8 cm (3 ⅛ in.); Diam. 5 cm (2 in.)
Rogers Fund, 1925 (25.3.282, 25.3.283)

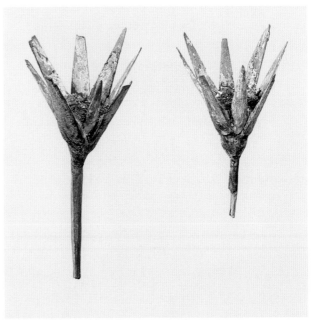

cat no. 43A, B

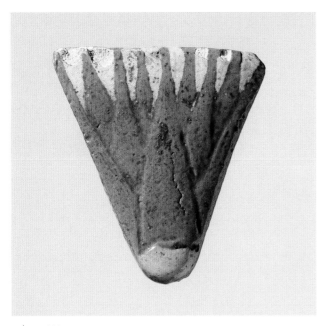

cat no. 44A

cat no. 44B

44. WATER LILY INLAYS

A. Dynasty 18, ca. 1400–1300 B.C.
Provenance unknown
Faience
4 x 3.6 x 0.5 cm (1⁹⁄₁₆ x 1⁷⁄₁₆ x ³⁄₁₆ in.)
Museum Accession (x.144.21)

B. Dynasty 18, ca. 1400–1300 B.C.
Amarna
Faience
3.7 x 3.4 x 0.5 cm (1⁷⁄₁₆ x 1⁵⁄₁₆ x ³⁄₁₆ in.)
Purchase, Edward S. Harkness Gift, 1926 (26.7.967)

The water lily, more commonly referred to as the lotus, was one of the most ubiquitous plants and symbols of ancient Egypt. Its flower, which is either blue or white (*Nymphaea coerulea* and *alba*), closes up at night and reopens in the morning to reveal a central yellow circle radiating yellow petals. To the ancient Egyptians this phenomenon reflected the rising of the sun at the dawn of creation, and the flower was honored as an image of daily rebirth and rejuvenation.

Depictions of the water lily, such as these models (cat. no. 43) and inlays (cat. no. 44), usually incorporate this symbolism, but the plant was also valued for its medicinal properties. Its root, which contains pain-relieving apomorphine alkaloids, was included in prescriptions for headaches, rashes and sores, stomach problems and constipation, and for a liver ailment. The Greek author Dioscorides (ca. A.D. 40–90) reported that the Egyptians also consumed the water lily cooked or raw and used its seeds in bread.

J P A and D T M

45–46. WATER LILY VESSELS

Dynasty 18, ca. 1400–1300 B.C.
Provenance unknown
Faience
H. 7.5 cm (3 in.); Diam. 17.7 cm (7 in.)
Rogers Fund, 1918 (18.2.6)

Dynasty 18, ca. 1500–1300 B.C.
Provenance unknown
Faience
H. 15 cm (5⅞ in.); Diam. 9 cm (3⁹⁄₁₆ in.)
Purchase, Edward S. Harkness Gift, 1926 (26.7.972)

The medicinal value of the water lily (see cat. nos. 43, 44) derives in part from the fact that its root acts as a mild analgesic (painkiller) when ingested. The Egyptians were undoubtedly aware of this property, and it may be reflected in the forms of these two vessels, which depict a water lily pad and flower.

The pad-shaped vessel (cat. no. 45) is in two pieces, with the lower part acting as a stand for the broad cup.

Containers of this type were used to hold perfumed oils applied by servants to guests at a banquet. The oils may have been prepared in part from the flower; since the water lily itself has little or no scent, however, its symbolism in this context may also reflect the plant's soothing quality. The purpose of the flower-shaped chalice is less certain. It is a relatively common type in the New Kingdom, so it was probably not designed specifically to hold an infusion made from the water lily. Instead, its symbolism may reflect an association either with the plant's analgesic properties, if it held wine, or with the water lily's aquatic habitat, if it served as a water glass.

JPA and DTM

cat. no. 45

BIBLIOGRAPHY
Cat. no. 46: H. Schäfer and W. Andrae, *Die Kunst des alten Orients,* Propyläen-Kunstgeschichte 2 (Berlin: Propyläen-Verlag, 1925), p. 411; G. Steindorff, *Die Kunst der Ägypter: Bauten–Plastik– Kunstgewerbe* (Leipzig: Insel-Verlag, 1928), p. 276.

cat. no. 45 (detail of interior)

cat. no. 46

47–48. TALL-NECKED JARS

Dynasty 18, ca. 1500–1400 B.C.
Thebes, Lower Asasif, Carter-Carnarvon Excavations, tomb 37
(burial 78)
Pottery
H. 14.5 cm (5¾ in.); Diam. 5.3 cm (2⅛ in.)
Rogers Fund, 1912 (12.181.263)

Dynasty 18, ca. 1500–1400 B.C.
Thebes, Lower Asasif, Carter-Carnarvon Excavations, tomb 37
(burial 78)
Pottery
H. 13.7 cm (5⅜ in.); Diam. 6.5 cm (2⁹⁄₁₆ in.)
Rogers Fund, 1912 (12.181.264)

Containers such as these, known as Cypriote Base-Ring I juglets, or "bilbils," were first imported into Egypt in the early Eighteenth Dynasty and are often found in modest burials. It has been suggested that the vessel's shape is modeled after the inverted seedpod of the opium poppy (*Papaver somniferum*) and served to advertise its contents: opium, a powerful sedative that can be used not only as a painkiller but also in the treatment of diarrhea, dysentery, fever, and similar complaints.[1] Many such examples have been tested for opium, but only one (which lacks an excavated provenance) has been demonstrated to have actually contained the substance.[2]

Although the jars may have entered Egypt containing opium, after use they were often filled with oils or ointments, resealed, and included in burials. Both of these examples were found in the coffin of a woman along with personal possessions such as jewelry, a kohl pot, an ointment jar made of Egyptian alabaster, and a wood comb. The association with opium (and its beneficial medicinal properties) may have been thought to transfer magically to the vessels' new contents for use by the deceased in the afterlife.

SJA

NOTES

1. R. S. Merrillees, "Opium Trade in the Bronze Age Levant," *Antiquity* 36 (1962), pp. 287–92; R. S. Merrillees, *The Cypriote Bronze Age Pottery Found in Egypt*, Studies in Mediterranean Archaeology 18 (Lund: Åström, 1968), pp. 154–55.

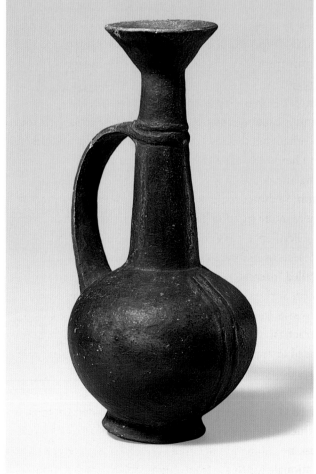

2. N. G. Bissett et al., "Was Opium Known in 18th Dynasty Ancient Egypt? An Examination of Materials from the Tomb of the Chief Royal Architect Kha," *Ägypten und Levante* 6 (1996), pp. 199–201; N. G. Bissett et al., "The Presence of Opium in a 3.500 Year Old Cypriote Base-Ring Juglet," *Ägypten und Levante* 6 (1996), pp. 203–4.

BIBLIOGRAPHY

Hayes, *Scepter* II, p. 209, fig. 123; R. S. Merrillees, *The Cypriote Bronze Age Pottery Found in Egypt,* Studies in Mediterranean Archaeology 18 (Lund: Åström, 1968), pp. 120–21, no. 5.

49–50. STATUES OF SEKHMET

Dynasty 18, reign of Amenhotep III, ca. 1390–1352 B.C.
Thebes
Diorite
210 x 47.5 x 95.5 cm (82 ¹¹⁄₁₆ x 18 ¹¹⁄₁₆ x 37 ⅝ in.)
Gift of Henry Walters, 1915 (15.8.2)

Dynasty 18, reign of Amenhotep III, ca. 1390–1352 B.C.
Thebes
Diorite
213 x 49.5 x 97.5 cm (83 ⅞ x 19 ½ x 38 ⅜ in.)
Gift of Henry Walters, 1915 (15.8.3)

The goddess Sekhmet represented the force of violence and unexpected disaster. Because these dangers often came from the animals and foreign inhabitants of Egypt's deserts, she was associated with the lion, the most common threat from this quarter in ancient times, and is usually depicted, as she is here, with the body of a woman and the head of a lion.[1] The sun disk and uraeus on her head derive from her association with the scorching and dehydrating qualities of the sun. But like the sun, Sekhmet could also bestow life, an aspect reflected here in the sign for "life" she holds in her left hand.

Pestilence was another threat originating in the deserts or in foreign lands (which the Egyptians also called "deserts"), and therefore it, too, was associated with Sekhmet, along with the general phenomenon of disease. In treating such illnesses with magic as well as practical means, the physicians of ancient Egypt saw the need to appease Sekhmet, and for that reason they were usually priests of the goddess (see cat. no. 57).

These statues are two of the more than seven hundred created during the reign of Amenhotep III, most of which were erected at Thebes in the temple of Mut (see cat. no. 26) and in the king's own mortuary temple. The rationale for this extraordinary and otherwise unparal-

cat. no. 49

leled production is unknown, but it may have been an attempt to ward off a series of epidemics that ravaged the Near East during the reign of Amenhotep III, or it could represent the pharaoh's thanksgiving for deliverance from these plagues.

NOTE

1. The male lion's head, with its distinctive mane, was used for both male and female deities associated with the lion, perhaps because it is more easily distinguished from the heads of other felines.

BIBLIOGRAPHY

Cat. nos. 49, 50: A. M. Lythgoe, "Statues of the Goddess Sekhmet," *BMMA* 14, part 2 (October 1919), p. 19, fig. 16, p. 17, fig. 14; *Cat. no. 49:* A. P. Kozloff, in *Egypt's Dazzling Sun: Amenhotep III and His World,* ed. A. P. Kozloff and B. Bryan, exh. cat. (Cleveland: Cleveland Museum of Art, 1992), pp. 225–26. *Cat. no. 50:* Hayes, *Scepter* II, p. 238 and fig. 143; J. Capart, *Pour faire aimer l'art égyptien* (Brussels: Fondation Égyptologique Reine Élisabeth, 1949), pp. 43–44, fig. 28; G. Steindorff and K. C. Seele, *When Egypt Ruled the East,* rev. ed. (Chicago: University of Chicago Press, 1957), p. 138, fig. 33.

51. LIBATION DISH

Dynasty 1, ca. 3100–2900 B.C.
Provenance unknown
Greywacke
17.5 x 14.5 x 2.5 cm (6⅞ x 5¹¹⁄₁₆ x 1 in.)
Rogers Fund, 1919 (19.2.16)

Experimentation in carving stone vessels reached its zenith in the Early Dynastic Period (Dynasty 1–2, ca. 3100–2650 B.C.), when craftsmen became highly successful at translating the plasticity associated with clay into forms made from soft stone such as greywacke. This spouted dish is an exquisite example of that artisinal skill. The piece incorporates two hieroglyphic symbols, a pair of arms ⊔ embracing an ankh ☥, the sign for "life." The vessel was designed so that the arms would envelop water poured into the dish. The liquid would then flow into the bowl-like portion of the ankh through several openings before being poured out through the spout in the lower portion of the ankh.

cat. no. 50

The ankh was undoubtedly intended to magically give force of life to water poured from the dish, turning it into a potent libation.[1] The precise meaning of the arms is less clear. They may have been meant to protect the water in the dish, but it is more likely that they have a hieroglyphic value, like the ankh. As a hieroglyph, the pair of arms represents the concept of *ka*, or "life force," which the Egyptians believed to be passed from the gods to people through an embrace. It may also be read as an abbreviated spelling of *kau*, or "nourishment," an abstract noun formed from the word *ka*. The integration of the concepts embodied in the pair of arms and the ankh reinforced the power of each sign. Thus, water poured from this dish would absorb life from the ankh, the ultimate form of sustenance required by the *ka*. Given the ancient Egyptian's propensity for using writing to communicate multiple meanings, it is quite likely more than one interpretation of the two signs was intended.

Predynastic examples (ca. 3600–3300 B.C.) of rough ceramic dishes with *ka* arms applied along their rims have been recovered from cemeteries, where they were employed in funerary rituals in which providing the deceased with food was essential.[2] This vessel's sophisticated symbolism and delicate quality, however, suggest that it was used in a temple cult.

DCP

NOTES

1. H. G. Fischer's study, "Some Emblematic Uses of Hieroglyphs with Particular Reference to an Archaic Ritual Vessel," *MMJ* 5 (1972), pp. 5–15, was the first to discuss this vessel in depth and provide a date.

2. E. R. Ayrton and W. L. S. Loat, *Pre-dynastic Cemetery at El Mahasna*, Memoir of the Egypt Exploration Fund 31 (London: Egypt Exploration Fund, 1911), pl. 26; M. A. Hoffman et al., *The Predynastic of Hierakonpolis: An Interim Report*, Egyptian Studies Association Publication 1 (Giza: Cairo University Herbarium, Faculty of Science; Macomb, Ill.: Western Illinois University, Department of Sociology and Anthropology, 1982), pl. I.2.

BIBLIOGRAPHY

Hayes, *Scepter* I, pp. 42–43, fig. 31; C. Aldred, *The Egyptians* (London: Thames and Hudson, 1961), p. 76, pl. 3; H. G. Fischer, "Some Emblematic Uses of Hieroglyphs with Particular Reference to an Archaic Ritual Vessel," *MMJ* 5 (1972), pp. 5–15, figs. 1–5; E. R. Russman, in "Egyptian Art," ed. C. Lilyquist, *BMMA* 41, no. 3 (Winter 1983–84), p. 4, fig. 2; A. P. Kozloff, in *Egypt's Dazzling Sun: Amenhotep III and His World*, ed. A. P. Kozloff and B. Bryan, exh. cat. (Cleveland: Cleveland Museum of Art, 1992), p. 321, fig. XI.2.

52. THE METTERNICH STELA

Dynasty 30, reign of Nectanebo II, 360–343 B.C.
Alexandria
Greywacke
83.5 x 33.5 x 14.4 cm (32⅞ x 13³⁄₁₆ x 5¹¹⁄₁₆ in.)
Fletcher Fund, 1950 (50.85)

One of the most perfectly preserved objects to have survived from ancient Egypt, this intricately carved and inscribed stela was originally erected in a temple of the Mnevis bull in Heliopolis during the reign of Nectanebo II by its donor, a priest of the temple named Esatum. It was probably removed in the Ptolemaic Period to Alexandria, where it was discovered at the beginning of the nineteenth century. In 1828 the ruler of Egypt, Muhammad Ali, gave it to the Austrian chancellor, Prince Metternich, and it remained in the Metternich family until shortly before its purchase by The Metropolitan Museum of Art.

Esatum's dedicatory inscription indicates that he commissioned the stela in part for the purpose of "giving air to the suffocating." Several of the stela's texts make clear that this refers to the perceived effects of scorpion stings or bites by poisonous snakes. The stela is covered with protective images and texts, and the Egyptians believed that water poured over it could absorb their efficacy and serve as a magical antivenom.

The stela's front, back, and sides are covered with images of protective deities, including Bes and Taweret. The most important of these is the scene in high relief on the front (p. 51), which shows the infant Horus protected by the head of Bes and Horus eyes (see cat. no. 16) as he subdues snakes, scorpions, a lion, and an oryx (all animals emblematic of the desert). To his left stands the god Thoth with the inscription: "Recitation by Thoth, lord of Hermopolis: I have come from the sky by command of the Sun so that I might make your protection at your bed day and night, and (for) any man who is suffering as well." To his right is Isis with the text: "Recitation by Isis the great, the god's mother: Don't fear, don't fear, my son Horus! I will be around you as your protection and drive away all evil from you and (from) any man who is suffering as well." These reflect the essential content of most of the stela's texts, which relate the story of how the infant Horus was cured of a poisonous bite by Thoth and Isis.

The six registers above this scene are centered on an image of the rising sun at top, which is labeled on both sides "Worshiping the Sun Harakhti, the great god, lord of the sky, variegated of plumage, who comes from the Akhet (the zone between the netherworld and the day sky)." To the left is an image of Thoth with the words: "Recitation: Thoth comes, arrayed with magic, to enchant poison—and it will not have control of any limb of the afflicted—as he enchants the rebels in the youngsters' room when they rebel against the Sun, continually forever." To the right the pharaoh Nectanebo is shown worshiping the sun; the text above him reads: "Recitation by the lord of the Two Lands, SENEDJEMIBRE-SETEPENAMUN: Oh, lord of fire, flame, and burning, give your firelight in my path and not your fire against me."

The king is also honored by inscriptions at the top of the back and on the top of the base on either side of the stela. On the back (p. 53, top) the central image is that of the setting sun, and the texts on either side of it read:

The western eye is filled with needed sustenance. The image has been set on his sacred seat, illuminating the west of the sky by rising on high in it. The gods' faces are big with the illumination of the living ba. As the Sun lives, the Dual King SENEDJEMIBRE-SETEPENAMUN lives, and vice versa. (right)

The eastern eye is filled with its perfection and regulated in every month and every half-month. He whose arms are complete about him is Shu lifting its boat and the stars and gods to their course. As it is sound, the Sun's son NECTANEBO is sound, and vice versa. (left)

Detail of front (top)

Horus. The story's setting is the marshes of Khemmis in the Nile Delta, where Isis hid with her newborn son to escape from Seth, who had killed her husband Osiris; an image of Isis nursing Horus in the marsh can be seen at the bottom of the scenes on the back and right side.

At the top of each side of the stela are twelve registers with deities similar to those on the back and front (p. 52). Each side text begins at the center of the top of the stela, skips these registers, and then continues below. Appendices to the tale on the base, they present a magic spell with which Thoth healed the injured Horus (right side, p. 59) and Thoth's invocation of the cured Horus to exercise his own magic on behalf of humans who are similarly afflicted (left side, p. 61). The latter ends with Horus's words "I am Horus the Savior," which echo the central image on the front of the stela.

The back of the stela (p. 62) is inscribed with a spell for protection of those traveling on the Nile, a second story set in the Delta marshes, and two spells to counter a scorpion sting and snakebite. The last two lines on the back contain Esatum's dedicatory inscription.

For the ancient Egyptians, these stories and spells constituted a powerful compendium of magic against two of their most pervasive threats, scorpions and snakes, whose stings and bites often caused injury or death. The stories are not mere tales but what is known as a "mythological precedent." Their description of the gods' own experience with overcoming these dangers gave a divine efficacy to the spells within the stories themselves and to those associated with the stories. Together with the stela's images of these gods and other protective forces, they were a powerful psychological weapon in the armarium of ancient Egyptian medicine.

The texts on top of the base at either side (p. 53, bottom) address the king with similar words: "Young god SENEDJEMIBRE-SETEPENAMUN, the Sun's son NECTANEBO, your protection is that of Horus the Savior, the great god, and vice versa" (left) and "Young god SENEDJEMIBRE-SETEPENAMUN, the Sun's son NECTANEBO, your protection is the gods' and goddesses' protection, and vice versa" (right).

The stela's texts read from the front to the base, then on either side, and conclude on the back. They begin with a magic spell against Apophis, the giant snake who inhabits the Duat (netherworld) and tries to impede the sun's voyage through it at night. That spell is followed by one against poison and three for healing a cat that has been poisoned by an insect or snakebite (p. 54). These spells end on the base (pp. 55–57), the remainder of which is inscribed with a story of Isis and the infant

BIBLIOGRAPHY
W. Golénischeff, *Die Metternichstele* (Leipzig: Englemann, 1877); N. E. Scott, "The Metternich Stela," *BMMA* 9 (1950–51), pp. 201–17; J. Yoyotte, "Prêtres et sanctuaires du nome héliopolite à la Basse Époque," *Bulletin de l'Institut Français d'Archéologie Orientale* 54 (1954), pp. 86–87; C. E. Sander-Hansen, *Die Texte der Metternichstele*, Analecta Aegyptiaca 7 (Copenhagen: Munksgaard, 1956); M.-L. Buhl, *The Late Egyptian Anthropoid Stone Sarcophagi*, Nationalmuseets skrifter, Arkæologisk-historisk række 6

Detail of left side (top)   Detail of right side (top)

(Copenhagen: Nationalmuseet, 1959), p. 165; H. G. Fischer, "Egyptian Turtles," *BMMA* 24 (1965–66), p. 200, fig. 13; H. G. Fischer, *Ancient Egyptian Representations of Turtles,* The Metropolitan Museum of Art Papers 13 (New York: MMA, 1968), p. 19, pl. 9; H. G. Fischer, "Some Emblematic Uses of Hieroglyphs with Particular Reference to an Archaic Ritual Vessel," *MMJ* 5

(1972), p. 8; L. Kákosy, "Metternichstele," in *Lexikon der Ägyptologie,* ed. W. Helck et al., vol. 4 (1982), pp. 122–23; P. Dorman, in "Egyptian Art," ed. C. Lilyquist, *BMMA* 41, no. 3 (Winter 1983–84), pp. 50–51; C. Jacq, *Egyptian Magic* (Warminster: Aris and Phillips; Chicago: Bolchazy-Carducci, 1985), p. 14, fig. 4; J.-C. Goyon, "Nombre et univers: Réflexions sur quelques données numériques

Detail of back (top)

de l'arsenal magique de l'Égypte pharaonique," in *La magia in Egitto ai tempi dei faraoni*, ed. A. Roccati and A. Siliotti (Milan: Rassegna Internazionale di Cinematografia Archeologica, Arte e Natura Libri, 1987), pp. 61–62, figs. 12, 13; P. Dorman, in *The Metropolitan Museum of Art: Egypt and the Ancient Near East*, ed. P. Dorman et al. (New York: MMA, 1987), pp. 80–81.

TRANSLATION

SPELL AGAINST APOPHIS (front)

Back, you, Apophis! You intestine of the Sun, you folding of the intestines, who has no arms, who has no legs, you have no body in which you have evolved. You whose tail is long within his cavern, you intestine, withdraw for the Sun! Your head has been severed, your (body's)

severance has been made, and you will not lift your face. His flame is in your *ba*, his butcher block's smell is in your flesh, and your form has been felled with the knife of the great God. Selket will do magic and deflect your strength. Stop, stop! Reverse through her magic!

SPELL AGAINST POISON (front)

Be spewed out, you poison! Come, come out on the ground! Now that Horus has enchanted you, constrained you, and spat on you, you cannot rise up, trampled down; weakened, you cannot grow forceful; become craven, you cannot fight; blind, you cannot see; your head turned upside down, you will not raise your face; reversed, you cannot find a way; saddened, you cannot become happy; lost, you cannot open your face— through what Horus, functional of magic, has said.

The poison that was active, for whom the heart of many became sad, Horus has killed it with his effective magic, and he who was in sadness is in joy. Stand up, you who are in sadness, for Horus has endowed you with life! He who came burdened has escaped by himself because of the felling of the biting rebels; every eye will glimpse the Sun and worship Osiris's son. Be turned, snake, and take that poison of yours that is in any limb of the afflicted! Look, the magic of Horus is forceful against you. You shall spew out, opponent. Be turned, you poison!

SPELLS FOR HEALING A CAT (front and base)

Spell for enchanting a cat. Recitation: O Sun, come for your daughter, for a scorpion has bitten her on the path

Detail of base (top of left side)

Detail of base (top of right side)

Detail of front (bottom)

alone! Her cry reaches above and is heard on your paths. Poison has entered her body and pervaded her flesh. It has given its mouth to her. Look, the poison is in her body. So come with your control, with your wrath, with your redness! Look, it is hidden before you, having entered in every limb of this cat I am treating.

Don't fear, don't fear, my effective daughter! Here I am around you. I am the one who fells for you the poison that is in any limb of this cat.

You cat, your head is the head of the Sun, the Two Lands' lord, who strikes disaffected subjects, fear of whom is in all lands and all the living forever. You cat, your eyes are the eye of the Effective Eye's owner, who illumines the Two Lands with his eye, who illumines the face in darkness's path. You cat, your nose is the nose of twice-great Thoth, lord of Hermopolis, chief of the Two Lands of the Sun, who gives air to the nose of every man. You cat, your ears are the ears of the Lord to the Limit, who hears the voice of every man when they call, who judges in the whole land. You cat, your mouth is the mouth of Atum, lord of life, the Unity: as he has

given unity, he has saved you from every poison. You cat, your neck is the neck of Ka-Assigner at the fore of the Big Enclave, who makes people live through his action. You cat, your front is the front of Thoth, lord of Maat, for he has given you air to let your throat breathe, and air has been given to its inside. You cat, your heart is the heart of Ptah, for he has ameliorated your heart from the bad poison that is in any limb of yours. You cat, your hands are the hands of the Big Ennead and the Little Ennead, for it has saved your hand from the poison of the mouth of every snake. You cat, your belly is the belly of Osiris, lord of Busiris; poison cannot do anything it wants to your belly. You cat, your thighs are Montu's thighs, for he has erected your thighs and gotten that poison down. You cat, your shins are the shins of Khonsu, who wanders the Two Lands every day and night, for he has made that poison flow down. You cat, your feet are the feet of Amun, the Great One, lord of Thebes: he has fixed your feet on the earth and felled that poison. You cat, your forearms are the forearm of Horus, who cares for his father Osiris, who gave Seth to the evil that he did. You cat, your soles are the soles of the Sun, for he has made that poison turn down. You cat, your inside is the inside of the Great Flood. That inside poison has been felled and constrained from every limb in you as the limb of the gods in the sky, as the limb of the gods in the earth. They have felled every poison in you. There is no limb in you free of a god.

Felled and constrained for her has been that poison of any male or female snake, any scorpion, or any crawling thing that is in any limb of this cat that is suffering. Look, now that Isis has spun and Nephthys has woven against that poison, this bandage shall be strong and this magic shall work through what the Sun Harakhti, the great god at the fore of the Dual Shrines, has said. You bad poison that is in any limb of this cat that is suffering, come, come down!

Another spell. Recitation: Sun, come to your daughter! Shu, come to your wife! Isis, come to your sister! Save her from that bad poison that is in any limb of hers! O you gods, come and fell that bad poison that is in any limb of this cat that is suffering!

Another spell like it. Don't fear, don't fear, Bastet, powerful of mind at the fore of the sacred marsh! You shall have control of all the gods, and no one can have control of you. Come out after my speech, you bad poison that is in any limb of the cat who is suffering!

Detail of base (top of front)

STORY OF ISIS AND THE INFANT HORUS (base)

I am Isis, who had conceived her baby and was pregnant with divine Horus. When I had given birth to Horus, Osiris's son, within the nest of Khemmis, I became agitated over it very much, saying: "Now that I have seen the one who will answer for his father, I will hide him and conceal him for fear of that evil one, and I will wander as a beggar in fear of the one who does violence and spend my time searching and acting on Horus's behalf."

When I returned to look for Horus, I found him, Horus, young and golden, a helpless and fatherless child, having wet the shores with the waters of his eye and the spittle of his lips, his body inert and his heart languid, and the vessels of his body not beating. I let out a wail, saying: "It is I, it is I," but the child was too weak to respond. My breasts were engorged and his belly empty, the mouth needing its thing. The well was brimful and the child thirsty, and my intention was to come to his aid, for he was greatly injured, but the child was helpless and refused the milk jug, having been left alone too long.

How great was the fear for lack of one to come at my voice! My father was in the Duat, my mother in the Place of Silence, and my elder brother in the sarcophagus. The other brother was the enemy, extensive in the fury of his heart against me, and my little sister was against me in his house. So who among people could I call to and their heart would turn to me? So I called to

Detail of base (front)

Detail of base (left side)

Khemmis cannot turn to him. Horus is safe from the evil of his brother and those in his (brother's) following cannot overthrow him. Seek out how this happened to him and Horus will live for his mother. Perhaps a scorpion was stinging him or a jealous snake poisoning him."

When Isis put her nose in his mouth and discovered the smell there as that of one within his sarcophagus, she recognized the illness of the god's heir, having found (him) to have poison. She embraced (him) very, very quickly, jumping around like fish thrown on a frying pan: "Horus has been bitten, Sun. Your son has been bitten. Horus has been bitten—the heir of your heir, who raises the kingship of Shu. Horus has been bitten—the youth of Khemmis, the child of the Official's Enclave. The young child of gold has been bitten, the helpless, fatherless baby. Horus has been bitten—Onnophris's son, to whom She Who Laments gave birth. Horus has been bitten—the innocent one, the youngest son among the gods. Horus has been bitten—whose care was entrusted to me with a view to answering for his father. Horus has been bitten—the one cared for in secret, feared in the belly of his mother. Horus has been bitten—the one I guarded from sight, for whose heart I desired life. The helpless one has been cheated of care, and those assigned to the child are powerless."

So Nephthys came, weeping, and her wail went around the marsh. Selket said: "What? What? Who now is against son Horus? Isis, call out to the above so that a

those in the marsh and they turned to me at once. The lowly came to me from their house and sprang to me at my voice. They mourned at it, saying how great was my suffering. But there was no one there who could enchant him with his spell, though every man of them was jabbering very, very much; there was none of them who knew a life-giving spell.

There came to me a woman wise in her town, a noblewoman at the fore of her district. More trustworthy than they because of her knowledge, she came to me with her mouth full of life: "Don't fear, don't fear, son Horus! Don't despair, don't despair, god's mother! The child is safe from the evil of his brother. The bush (where he lies) is hidden and the Captive cannot enter it. The magic of Atum, the gods' father, who is in the sky, is your life-maker. Seth cannot enter this district and

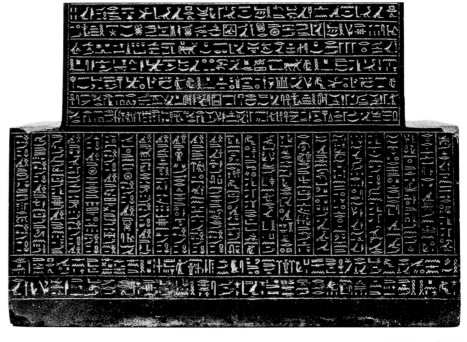

Detail of base (back)

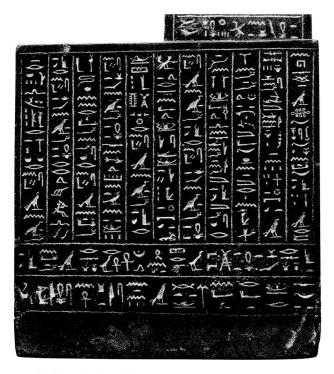

Detail of base (right side)

strike will happen in the Sun's crew and the boat of the Sun cannot proceed while son Horus is (ill) on his side." Isis sent her voice above, her cry to the boat of Millions, and the sun disk landed opposite her and did not move from his place.

Thoth came, equipped with his magic and bearing the great command of justification. "What, what, Isis the goddess, effective one who knows her mouth? There can be no evil against son Horus: his protection is that of the boat of the Sun. I have come today from the god's boat. The sun disk is in its place of yesterday; darkness has happened and sunlight is repelled until Horus gets well for his mother Isis—and every man who is suffering as well."

Isis the goddess spoke: "Thoth, how great is your intention, but your plan for it is too late. Though you have come equipped with your magic and bearing the great command of justification, one thing after another without number, look, Horus is in need because of poison. The evil is so bad that the needy one will die completely. Would that he were again united with his mother and I would not see this hounding him. My mind would be at rest from it. From the first I hesitated to respond, 'Horus, Horus, stay on earth!' From the day I got him I have wished to bestow the life force of his father, but the child is ill."

"Don't fear, don't fear, Isis the goddess! Nephthys, don't wail! I have come from the sky with the air of life to make the child live for his mother. Horus, your heart is firm: it cannot grow weary because of the fire.

"Horus's protection is the one in his sun disk, when he has ignited the Two Lands with the effectiveness of his two eyes—and the protection of the afflicted as well. Horus's protection is the eldest in Nut, who commands the conduct of what is and what is not—and the protection of the afflicted as well. Horus's protection is that big dwarf who goes around the Two Lands at twilight—and the protection of the afflicted as well. Horus's protection is the lion by night, who sails at the fore of the western mountain—and the protection of the afflicted as well. Horus's protection is the big hidden ram, who goes around in his sacred eyes—and the protection of the afflicted as well. Horus's protection is the large falcon who hovers in the sky, earth, and Duat—and the protection of the afflicted as well. Horus's protection is the august beetle with large wings at the fore of the Duat—and the protection of the afflicted as well. Horus's protection is the secret corpse in his mummy within his sarcophagus—and the protection of the afflicted as well. Horus's protection is the Duat-dweller of the Two Lands, who goes around in faces, secret of properties—and the protection of the afflicted as well. Horus's protection is the divine heron, who climbs within his sacred eyes—and the protection of the afflicted as well. Horus's protection is his own body and the magic of his mother Isis is his protection. Horus's protection is the identities of his father in his conduct in the nomes—and the protection of the afflicted as well. Horus's protection is the mourning of his mother and the cries of his brothers—and the protection of the afflicted as well. Horus's protection is his own identity, which the gods serve by aiding him—and the protection of the afflicted as well.

"Be awake, Horus, for your protection is set, and ease the mind of your mother Isis. Horus's voice will raise hearts when he has calmed her who was in sadness. Let your heart be sweet, you in Nut, for Horus has cared for his father.

"Retreat, poison! Look, you are enchanted by the mouth of Isis and the tongue of the great god has barred you. The boat is stopped and will not sail and the sun disk is where it was yesterday until Horus gets well for his mother Isis, until the afflicted gets well for his mother as well. Come down, so that the boat can proceed and Nut's crew can sail! Food will be marooned and the sanctuary closed up until Horus gets well for his mother Isis, until the afflicted gets well for his mother as well. Suffering will hurt those who have it and chaos will revert to its activity of yesterday until Horus gets well for his mother Isis, until the afflicted gets well for his mother as well. Harm will circulate, the times of day cannot be separated, light cannot be distinguished from shadow by day or night, until Horus gets well for his mother Isis, until the afflicted gets well for his mother as well. The two caverns will be closed up, vegetation will dry up, and life will retreat from the living, until Horus gets well for his mother Isis, until the afflicted gets well for his mother as well. Come down, poison, so that minds may become glad and sunlight may circulate! I am Thoth, the eldest son of the Sun, and Atum and the Ennead have commanded me to heal Horus for his mother Isis, and to heal the afflicted as well.

"Horus, Horus, your life force is your protection and your conduct is helping you. The poison is dead and its heat repelled because it has bitten the Powerful One's son. So, proceed to your homes: Horus is alive for his mother, and the afflicted as well."

Isis spoke: "So, may you reveal him to those in Khemmis and the nurses in Pe and Dep, and order them very, very much to keep the child sound for his mother, and to keep the afflicted sound as well. Don't let them think my life force in Khemmis was only that of a poor woman who fled her town."

Thoth spoke to the gods and told those in Khemmis: "Oh, nurses in Pe, who are beating themselves and flailing with their arms over that great one who has emerged at their fore, you shall watch over this child, seeking his way among faces. Divert the paths of those who rebel against him until he has acquired the Two Lands' throne. The Sun in the sky is responsible for him and his father is made watchful over him. The magic spells of his mother are his protection, circulating love of him and putting fear of him in faces. I am awaited to command the Nightboat and let the Dayboat proceed. Horus is yours, allotted to life. I shall report for the life to his father and give joy to those in the Nightboat so that the crew will sail—that Horus is alive for his mother Isis, and that the afflicted one is alive for his mother as well. That poison is powerless, so the expert will be blessed for his duty, for making report to the one

who sent him: 'Let your heart be glad, Sun Harakhti! Your son Horus is allotted to life.'"

THOTH'S SPELL FOR HORUS (top and right side)

You who are in the hole, you who are in the hole, you who are in the mouth of the hole! You who are in the path, you who are in the path, you who are in the mouth of the path! Mnevis, who will go to every man and every animal as well, *he* is a centipede who is off to Heliopolis, *he* is a scorpion who is off to the Elder's Enclave. You cannot bite him: *he* is the Sun. You cannot sting him: *he* is Thoth. You cannot shoot your poison at him: *he* is Nefertem. Every male and female serpent and every insect who bite with their mouth and sting with their tail, you cannot bite him with your mouth, you cannot sting him with your tail. You shall be far from him, you cannot make your fiery breath against him: *he* is Osiris's son. You shall spew out, you shall spew out, you shall spew out, you shall spew out!

I am Thoth. I have come from the sky to make protection of Horus and to bar the poison of the scorpion that is in any limb of Horus.

You have your head, Horus: it will be continually fixed with the crown. You have your eye, Horus: you are Horus, Geb's son, lord of the two eyes within the Ennead. You have your nose, Horus: you are Horus the Elder, the Sun's son, and you cannot inhale hot air. You have your upper arm, Horus: your strength is great enough to kill your father's opponents. You have your lower arms, Horus: you shall receive the office of your father Osiris, for Ptah has judged you on the day you were born. You have your chest, Horus: the sun disk is making your protection. You have your eye, Horus: your right eye is Shu, your left eye is Tefnut; they are the children of the Sun. You have your belly, Horus: the gods' children who are in it cannot receive the water of the scorpion. You have your rear, Horus: the strength of Seth cannot come about against you. You have your penis, Horus: you are his mother's bull, who cares for his father, who is responsible for his children in the course of every day. You have your thighs, Horus: thus your strength is to kill your father's opponents. You have your shins, Horus, that Khnum built, swaddled by Isis. You have your feet, Horus: the Nine Bows have been spread fallen under your feet, for you have managed the south, the north, the west, and the east. You are seen to be like the Sun, you are seen to be like the Sun, you are seen to

Detail of top (right side)

Detail of right side (bottom)

be like the Sun, you are seen to be like the Sun—and the afflicted as well.

THOTH'S INVOCATION OF HORUS (top and left side)
Horus was bitten in the marsh of Heliopolis, north of Vulva-town while his mother Isis was in the upper houses giving cool water to her brother Osiris. Horus sent his voice to the sun and He in the Rising heard (saying): "So, spring up at Horus's voice, keeper of the doors in the noble *ished* tree! Command mourning for him, command the sky to heal Horus and care for him with life! Have (Thoth), my *Isden* who is in Builder's Mound, told: 'Are you sleeping? Enter to the lord of sleep, for my son Horus is being squeezed, for my son Horus is being squeezed, and get everything to cut the poison that is in any limb of Horus, Isis's son—and that is in any limb of the afflicted as well.'"

Worshiping Horus to cure him by effective magic. To be said on water or on land. Recitation by Thoth, the savior of this god: "Greetings, god, son of a god! Greetings, heir, son of an heir! Greetings, bull, son of a bull, to whom a divine vulva gave birth! Greetings,

Horus, who came from Osiris, to whom divine Isis gave birth! I have recited with your magic, I have spoken with your effectiveness, I have enchanted with your words that your mind created. They are your spells that came from your mouth, that your father Geb commanded for you, that your mother Nut gave to you, that your incarnation Foremost of Letopolis taught, to make your protection, to repeat your aid, to seal the mouth of every crawling thing in the sky or in the earth or in the water, to give life to people, to content the gods, and to glorify the Sun with your praises.

"Come to me quickly, quickly, on this day as he who rows in the god's boat did for you, and bar for me every lion on the desert edge, every crocodile on the river, every biting mouth in their cavern, and make them for me like a pebble of the desert cliff, like a potsherd strewn in the street, and remove for me the flowing poison that is in any limb of the afflicted. Let your words not be scorned because of it. Look, your name has been called upon on this day. May you bring about awe of you, elevated for you by your effectiveness, and give life for me to the one who is being asphyxiated, and praise will be given you by the subjects, double Maat will be worshiped in your form, and every god will be summoned like you. Look, your name has been called upon on this day."

I am Horus the Savior.

SPELL FOR PROTECTION ON WATER (back)

Oh, elder one who rejuvenates himself at his time, long-lived one who makes his youth, may you make Thoth come to me at my voice and make Wild-Face retreat for me when Osiris is on the water, Horus's eye with him, and the great Scarab spread over him. You elder one with his fist, who gave birth to the gods as a child, may he who is on the water come out sound. If one approaches that which is on the water, one approaches Horus's weeping eye.

Back, you fish and crocodiles in the water, you dead man or woman, male or female opposition, and so forth! Don't lift your face, you fish and crocodiles in the water, until Osiris has passed by you! Look, he is bound for Busiris: let the mouth become small and your maw plugged.

Back, you rebel! Don't lift your face to him who is on the water—*they* are Osiris—for the Sun has risen to his boat to see the Ennead of Battleground; the Duat's lords are waiting to kill you. If Wild-Face comes to Osiris while he is on the water, Horus's eye is on him to capsize your face so that you are put on your back.

O, you fish and crocodiles in the water, your mouth has been shut by the Sun, your maw has been plugged by Sekhmet, your tongue has been cut out by Thoth, your eyes have been blinded by Magic. Those four great gods who make protection over Osiris, they are the ones who make protection for all people who are on the

water and all animals who are on the water on this day, who protect those in the water, who protect the sky and the Sun inside it, who protect the great god within the sarcophagus, who protect the one on the water. A great crying sound is in Neith's Enclave, a high sound is in the Great Enclave, a great moan is in the mouth of the cat. The gods and goddesses are saying: "Look, look, at the *abd* fish being born!"

Withdraw for me your tread, rebel! I am Khnum, lord of Antinoe. Beware of repeating injury a second time, because of what has been done to you before the Big Ennead. Be barred and withdraw for me! I am the god: "Hey, hey," he says. Have you not heard the great crying sound since nightfall on the shore of Nedit, the great crying sound of all the gods and every goddess as mourning for the violence you have done, evil rebel? Look, the Sun has stormed with rage over it and commanded that your cutting up be made. Back, rebel! Hey, hey!

STORY OF ISIS AND THE NOBLEWOMAN (back)

I am Isis. I came out of the weaving house that my brother Seth had put me in and Thoth, the elder god, chief of Maat in the sky and earth, spoke to me: "Come, Isis, goddess, for it is good to hear. One will live when another leads him. So hide with the baby son, that he may come to us when his body has grown and all his strength has evolved, and he may be made to rest on his throne when the office of the Two Lands' ruler has been acknowledged his."

I went out at the time of evening, and seven scorpions went out behind me that they might serve me: Tefen and Befen on both sides of me; Mestet and Mestefet under my bed; Petet, Tjetet, and Matet sweeping the way for me. I ordered them very, very (strongly), and my speech proceeded into their ears: "Don't know the black, don't ask the red, don't recognize the upper-class man from the lower-class. Keep your face down on the path; beware of letting him who seeks me go before we have reached Persui, the town of the two sisters at the front of the marsh and the rear of Buto."

And when I reached the houses of married women, a noblewoman saw me on the way and shut her doors on me, since she was upset at those who were with me. They consulted about her and put their poison together on the tip of the stinger of Tefen. A lowly woman opened her doorway to me so that her humble house could be entered, and Tefen entered under the door-

Detail of top (left side)

Detail of left side (bottom)

leaves of the (rich woman's) doorway and stung the rich woman's son. Fire broke out in the rich woman's house and there was no water there to quench it; the sky rained on the rich woman's house though it was not the season for it—for she did not open to me. Her heart became sad, since it was not known whether he would live. When she went around her town wailing in grief, there was no one who came at her voice.

My heart became sad for the little one because of her, enough to give life to the innocent one. I called to her, say-ing: "Come to me, come to me! Look, my mouth has life. I am a knowledgeable daughter of her town, who can repel the scurrying serpent with her utterance, for my father has taught me to know. I am his beloved, bodily daughter."

Isis laid her hands on the child to give life to the one being asphyxiated (saying): "Tefen's poison, come! Come out on the ground! You shall not course, you shall not enter. Befnet's poison, come! Come out on the ground! I am Isis the goddess, mistress of magic, doer of magic, effective of recitations: every biting serpent-mouth listens to me. You have fallen down, poison of Mestet; you cannot run, poison of Mestefet; you cannot

rise, poison of Petet and Tjetet; you cannot proceed, Matet. Fall down, mouth of the biter, for Isis has spoken, the goddess great of magic at the fore of the gods, to whom Geb has given his effectiveness to bar poison with her control. Be barred! Reverse! Retreat! Back, poison! Don't spring up! So says the Sun's beloved, egg of the goose who came from the sycamore.

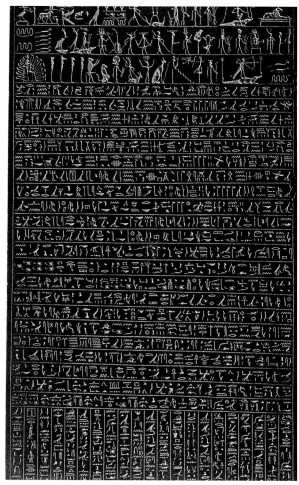

Detail of back (top)

Detail of back (bottom)

Now look, my words have been commanded since nightfall. I speak to you, I alone. Don't pull down our names throughout the nomes. Don't acknowledge the black, don't ask the red, don't look at the noblewomen in their houses. Keep your face down on the path until we reach the hiding place in Khemmis. Oh, may the child live and the poison die, may the Sun live and the poison die: then Horus will become healthy for his mother Isis, then he who is suffering will become healthy as well."

The fire was quenched, the sky grew calm at the utterance of Isis the goddess. The rich woman came and brought me her property; she filled the house of the lowly woman with food for the lowly child, for her door had been opened to me while the rich woman was upset. She went around in the night alone and bitter, her son was bitten, and the lowly woman got her property—as the result of her not opening to me.

Oh, may the child live and the poison die: then Horus will become healthy for his mother Isis, then everyone who is suffering will become healthy as well. Bread of emmer is what will repel poison so that it retreats; the fiery bulbs of onion is what will repel fever from the body.

SPELL AGAINST A SCORPION STING (back)
"Isis, Isis, come to your Horus! You who know her spell, come to your son," so say the gods in her area, "since a scorpion has stung him, a spiny scorpion has hunted him, an insect has rubbed him."

Isis came, a mesh shirt on her chest, having spread her arms. "Here I am, here I am, my son Horus. Don't fear, don't fear, you Effective One's son! Nothing evil will happen to you. The water of him who made what exists is in you. You are the son of the one in the midst of the Beaten Path, who came from Nu: you will not die from the heat of that poison. You are the big heron that was

62

born on top of the reeds in the great Official's Enclave in Heliopolis. You are the brother of the *abd* fish that foretells what happens. Since the cat has nursed you inside Neith's Enclave, with the hippopotamus sow and the female Bes as protection for your body, your head will not fall to one who crosses you, your body will not receive the heat of your poison, you will not turn back on land, you have not become wretched on water, no biting serpent-mouth will have control of you, no lion will exercise control of you. You are the son of the sacred god who came from Geb: you are Horus, and the poison will not have control of your body. You are the son of the sacred god who came from Geb—and the afflicted as well—and 4 noble goddesses are protection for your body.

SPELL AGAINST POISON (back)

He rises from the Akhet, sets into the Duat, and comes into being in the Height Enclave. He opens his eye and light happens, he closes it and darkness happens. The inundation is in accordance with his command; the gods will never learn his identity.

I am he who illumines the Two Lands, drives away darkness, and rises day and night. I am the bull of the eastern horizon, the lion of the western horizon, who crosses the above day and night without being repulsed. I have come at the voice of my daughter Isis: "Look, the bull has been bitten." The plait-snake is blinded: you poison, retreat from every limb of the afflicted; come on the ground! The afflicted is not the one you have bitten: Min, lord of Coptos, the child of the white sow that is in Heliopolis, is the one who has been bitten. Oh, Min, lord of Coptos, give air to the afflicted and you will be given air."

DEDICATION (back)

The god's-father and servant of the Lord of Existence, Esatum, son of the god's-father and servant of the Lord of Existence and scribe of the inundation, Ankh-Psamtik, whom the housemistress Tahatnub made, was the one who renewed this writing after he found it absent from the house of Osiris Mnevis, for the sake of making his mother's name live, forestalling for her death and every divine pain, and giving air to the suffocating, and for the sake of making live the families of all the gods. Then his lord Osiris Mnevis was heightening his lifetime with sweetness of mind and a final burial after old age because of this which he has done for the house of Osiris Mnevis.

53. CIPPUS

Ptolemaic Period, ca. 300–30 B.C.
Provenance unknown
Schist
20.3 x 13.4 x 5 cm (8 x 5¼ x 2 in.)
Rogers Fund, 1920 (20.2.23)

The Metternich Stela (cat. no. 52) is the largest and most elaborate example of a genre of Egyptian art known as cippi (singular cippus), which display an image of the infant Horus subduing dangerous animals. This small stela, though less grand, is more representative of the genre as a whole. It bears essentially the same central representation of Horus found on the Metternich Stela and is inscribed with similar images and texts. On the front the infant Horus the Savior is surrounded by various protective deities; the scene at the top of the back shows the winged sun disk accompanied by nine gods.

The stela's main text is a spell for protection on water, which is also found on the back of the Metternich Stela. Here it begins on the top and sides, continues on the back, and ends on the bottom of the base. The content

of the text indicates that the stela was intended primarily for protection rather than as a means of charging water poured over it with curative power, as was the Metternich Stela. Nevertheless, the vertical texts on either side of the central image of Horus, taken from the longer spells on the top and sides of the Metternich Stela, suggest that this stela, too, was used to transform water into a curative libation.

54. CIPPUS AMULET

Late Period–Early Ptolemaic Period, ca. 500–200 B.C.
Provenance unknown
Anhydrite
3.8 x 2.3 x 1.5 cm (1½ x ⅞ x ⅝ in.)
Rogers Fund, 1957 (57.143)

Although many cippi were made in the form of stelae (cat. nos. 52, 53), others were fashioned as small plaques or amulets and were meant to be carried or worn on the body. This amulet, carved with the same central image of the infant Horus found on all cippi, served to guard its wearer from poisonous snakes and insects. In the event of a mishap, it could also be immersed in water to provide an immediate antivenom.

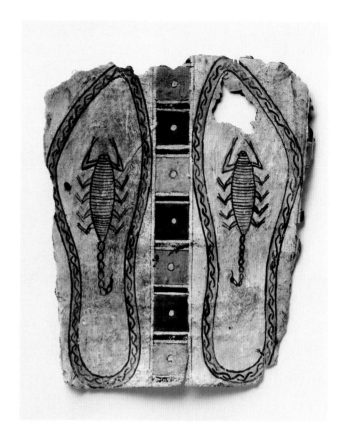

55. MUMMY FOOT PANEL

Roman Period, 1st–2nd century A.D.
Provenance unknown
Cartonnage and paint
36.5 x 22.2 cm (14⅜ x 8¾ in.)
Museum Accession (OC 328)

One of the first objects in the Metropolitan Museum's Egyptian collection, this panel once adorned the exterior foot end of a wrapped mummy. It depicts the soles of two sandals with a scorpion crushed beneath each one. The imagery reflects the ancient Egyptians' desire to control the dangerous elements of their world, a concern that here is transferred to the world of the afterlife. On the mummy, the scene was intended to give power to the deceased over the inimical forces that he would encounter on his nightly journey through the netherworld toward rebirth each dawn.

56. OINTMENT JAR

Dynasty 25, ca. 700 B.C.
Provenance unknown
Egyptian alabaster
H. 47 cm (18½ in.); Diam. 34 cm (13⅜ in.)
Rogers Fund, 1942 (42.2.2)

The incised inscription on this large jar identifies the contents of the vessel as "Special ointment of the Manager of the Red-Crown Enclaves and Chief Physician, Harkhebi." The man to whom the jar belonged probably lived in the Delta town of Buto; the "Red-Crown Enclaves" was an ancient area of that town, and his name, which means "Horus of Khemmis," refers to the site near Buto where the infant Horus was hidden by his mother, Isis (see cat. no. 52).

Ointments are frequently cited in medical papyri as a component in prescriptions (see cat. no. 60), and the contents of this jar may have been employed by Harkhebi for that purpose. It is also possible that the jar was made for the physician's tomb, but this is less likely, since Harkhebi's name lacks the epithet "justified," which was usually appended to the name of the deceased.

57. STATUE OF YUNY

Dynasty 19, reigns of Seti I to Ramesses II, ca. 1290–1260 B.C.
Asyut
Limestone
129 x 55 x 90.5 cm (50¾ x 21⅝ x 35⅝ in.)
Rogers Fund, 1933 (33.2.1)

This magnificent piece of early Ramesside art is one of two statues of Yuny found in or near the tomb-chapel of his father, the chief physician Amenhotep, in the New Kingdom necropolis of Asyut, Medjdeni (modern Deir Durunka). Yuny probably commissioned the chapel after his father's death. His own burial place is unknown, but it was most likely in the same complex. An inscription on the statue's base indicates that it was made for Yuny "according to his living image" by Yuny's assistant, whose name is lost.

Yuny, shown kneeling, is dressed in the robe, wig, and sandals of a nobleman. His eyes and eyebrows, originally made as inlays, are now lost. Between his knees and outstretched arms Yuny holds a shrine with a figure of the god Osiris. Reliefs and inscriptions below the shrine are those of a priest libating and offering to the god in the role of Osiris's grandson, Imseti; a table of the offerings is inscribed between the two figures of the priest.

Graffiti on the walls of Amenhotep's chapel show that the tomb was a place of pilgrimage in the Ramesside period, perhaps by visitors seeking the intercession of Yuny's father in healing ailments (see cat. no. 58). Although Yuny himself is not called "physician" or "chief physician" on his monuments, he probably followed his father in that occupation, as he did in most of his other offices. On this statue he has the title "overseer of Sekhmet's lay-priests," which indicates his association with the medical profession (see cat. nos. 49, 50, and 60).

The statue is inscribed on its base, back pillar, and shrine. Several of the inscriptions on the sides of the shrine are incomplete; rather than adjust the texts to fit the available space, the sculptor carved them as if they are covered by Yuny's hands and kilt. Yuny's wife, Renutet, is shown on both sides of the statue's back pillar.

In addition to the dedicatory inscription mentioned above, the statue's texts contain Yuny's titles, name, parentage, and an appeal to visitors as well as several of his addresses to Osiris, Onnophris (a form of Osiris), and other gods of Asyut. In most of these, Yuny is described as "justified," an epithet usually applied to the deceased. This and the content of the texts suggests that the statue was made after Yuny's death, perhaps to serve, in its own right, as an intermediary for visitors to his father's tomb complex.

BIBLIOGRAPHY
A. Kamal, "Fouilles à Deir Dronka et à Assiout (1913–1914)," *Annales du Service des Antiquités de l'Égypte* 16 (1916), pp. 86–89; H. E. Winlock, "Recent Purchases of Egyptian Sculpture," *BMMA* 29 (1934), pp. 184–85, fig. 1; Hayes, *Scepter* II, p. 351, fig. 219; K. A. Kitchen, *Ramesside Inscriptions, Historical and Biographical*, vol. 1 (Oxford: Blackwell, 1975), pp. 352–55; K. A. Kitchen, "Encore la famille de Iouny," *Revue d'égyptologie* 28 (1976), pp. 156–57; K. A. Kitchen, "Documentation additionnelle sur Iouny," *Revue d'égyptologie* 30 (1978), p. 168; P. Dorman, in *The Metropolitan Museum of Art: Egypt and the Ancient Near East*, ed. P. Dorman et al. (New York: MMA, 1987), pp. 68–69.

TRANSLATION

BASE (front)
Chief king's scribe Yuny, justified, says: "Oh lay-priests, lector-priests, god's-fathers, and every scribe experienced [in . . .], who know the script of Thoth! Your body's

health for the future, the lifetime of your contentment, and the placing of a tomb in your town will be in accordance with your [saying to] me 'May you wake [in] peace at the time of morning' and your saying to me 'May [your] *ba* live, may Onnophris give you a pure royal offering and air to your nose.'"

BASE (left side and back)
Member of the elite, high official, royal sealer, unique associate, dignitary, district administrator, royal scribe, chief lector-priest, overseer of Sekhmet's lay-priests, who knows the secret of the chest of Bubastis, *sem*-priest of the young god, who leads the festival of all the gods, royal scribe Yuny, justified, whom the dignitary, royal scribe, and chief physician Amenhotep, justified, engendered.

BASE (right side)
May every festival of the sky and of the earth be for the royal scribe and chief lector-priest Yuny, justified. The statue was made for him according to his living image, in order to rest in his enclave, by his assistant, temple-scribe [. . .].

BACK PILLAR
A royal offering of Thoth, lord of hieroglyphs, lord of Hermopolis, foremost of Heseret, at home in the Trap Enclave: may you give effectiveness, power, justification, cool water that comes from Nu, and clean bread of the Bas of Heliopolis to the royal scribe and chief lector-priest Yuny, that he may become justified through them, powerful through them, and stable through them forever.

A royal offering of Khnum, ruler of Hypselis, and Wepwawet, manager of the Nile Valley: may you both let the royal scribe and chief lector-priest Yuny, justified, be one of the crew in the following of Onnophris, that he may become justified through them and take things from the great purifications forever.

BACK PILLAR (right and left sides)
The one honored with Hathor, mistress of Medjdeni, his sister and beloved, the chantress of Wepwawet, Renutet, justified.

The one honored by the great god, his beloved sister, the chantress of Hathor of Medjdeni and housemistress, Renutet.

SHRINE (front)

[A royal offering of . . . by . . .] Yuny, justified, who says: "May you put me in your following forever." *(right)*

A royal offering of Osiris, Foremost of Westerners, by the royal scribe, chief lector-priest, and overseer of Sekhmet's lay-priests, Yuny, justified, who says: "May you put me in your mountain forever." *(left)*

SHRINE BASE (front)[1]

Making a royal offering by Imseti for his father Osiris, 4 times. *(right)*

Making purification by Imseti for his father Osiris, 4 times. *(left)*

SHRINE (right side)

Royal scribe and chief lector-priest Yuny, justified, says: "Oh, [. . .], I [will not . . .], I will not rob, I will not do wrong. May you put me among those westerners of justification forever." *(top, front, and base)*

Chief royal scribe and steward Yuny says: "Oh, all you gods of Atfet! May you let my place of the future be firm *(gap)* continually, while I am in the Lord of Life. May *(gap)* rest inside it, and my ba come upon earth to the place of yesterday." *(top and back)*

The one honored with Duamutef, the chief royal scribe Yuny, justified. The one honored with Qebehsenuef, the chief royal scribe Yuny, justified. The one honored *(sic)*. *(horizontals)*

SHRINE (left side)

Chief royal scribe Yuny, justified, says: "Greetings, Foremost of Westerners, Onnophris at home in the Abydene nome! I have come to you that I might do for you what is right, for I know that you partake of it. May you let me be justified forever." *(top, front, and base)*

Chief royal scribe Yuny, justified, says: "Greetings, lord of the Sacred Land and Ruler of the future *(gap)* continually! May you let" *(sic)*. *(top and back)*

The one honored with Imseti, the Osiris chief king's scribe Yuny. The one honored with Hapi, the Osiris chief king's scribe Yuny, justified. The one honored wi *(sic)*. *(horizontals)*

NOTE

1. The offering list includes quantities of oil, incense, poultry, beef, bread, beer, cool water, wine, milk, vegetables, grains, fruit, linen, and clothing.

58. PORTRAIT HEAD

Dynasty 30, reign of Nectanebo II, 360–343 B.C.
Provenance unknown
Basalt
21.2 x 14.5 x 16.2 cm (8⅜ x 5¹¹⁄₁₆ x 6⅜ in.)
Gift of Norbert Schimmel Trust, 1989 (1989.281.102)

This striking head depicts an elderly man whose face is marked by the lines, wrinkles, and sagging skin of old age. It is one of the earliest examples of sculpture that depicts the subject in an intensified, realistic manner. The style is similar to that of veristic portraits from the era of the Roman republic, in which every line and wrinkle of the subject's face is rendered. Typically Egyptian in this head, however, is the benevolent serenity with which the man contemplates the world. Similar pieces indicate that the statue to which it once belonged was that of a figure dressed in a long robe and a shoulder-length "bag" wig and holding a large cippus (see cat. nos. 52–54) in front of him: a genre of sculpture known as a "healing statue." Erected in a temple precinct, it was an object of pilgrimage for visitors suffering from various ailments. As with the Metternich Stela, pilgrims would pour water over the statue—in some instances the statue's base has a receptacle for collecting the libation—and then drink it as a cure for snakebites, scorpion stings, and other ailments. Both the wig and the robe were covered with magic spells like those inscribed on cippi, the remains of which can be seen on the front and right side of this head. The man depicted was probably a priest, like the donors of the Metternich Stela and other similar statues. There is no information whether he was also a physician, but for the Egyptians his statue itself would have served that function.

DA and JPA

BIBLIOGRAPHY

L. Kákosy, "Le statue magiche Guaritrici: Some Problems of the Magical Healing Statues," in *La magia in Egitto ai tempi dei faraoni*, ed. A. Roccati and A. Siliotti (Milan: Rassegna Internazionale di Cinematografia Archeologica, Arte e Natura Libri, 1987), p. 175; B. V. Bothmer, "Egyptian Antecedents of Roman Republican Verism," *Quaderni de 'La ricerca scientifica'* 116 (1988), pp. 60–62, pls. 9–11, reprinted in *Egyptian Art: Selected Writings of Bernard V. Bothmer*, ed. M. E. Cody (New York: Oxford University Press, 2004), pp. 418–19, 422–25; C. H. Roehrig, "Head of a Priest," in "Ancient Art: Gifts from the Norbert Schimmel Collection," *BMMA* 49, no. 4 (Spring 1992), p. 35.

59. STATUE OF IMHOTEP

Ptolemaic Period, ca. 300–30 B.C.
From the Nile Delta
Bronze, gold, and silver inlay
14 x 4.8 x 9.8 cm (5 ½ x 1 ⅞ x 3 ⅞ in.)
Purchase, Edward S. Harkness Gift, 1926 (26.7.852)

Imhotep was a high priest of Heliopolis and chief lector-priest at the beginning of Egypt's Third Dynasty (ca. 2650–2600 B.C.). He was also in charge of royal building projects, and in that capacity he probably oversaw the construction of the Step Pyramid complex of

King Djoser, the world's first monumental structure in stone. The significance of this accomplishment made such an impression on the Egyptians that Imhotep was remembered and honored for the remainder of ancient Egyptian civilization. Beginning in the New Kingdom he was invoked as the patron of writing and wisdom, and by the time this statue was made he had achieved fully divine status, with his own mythology and cult.

Perhaps because of his reputation for wisdom, Imhotep was also invoked for his intercession in sickness and infertility, and he was later equated by the Greeks with their own god of medicine, Asklepios. This statue shows Imhotep in his traditional pose, seated on a chair with a papyrus scroll unfolded on his lap. It may have been dedicated to him to seek his aid in a medical problem.

60. THE EDWIN SMITH PAPYRUS

Dynasty 16–17, ca. 1600 B.C.
Thebes
Papyrus and ink
L. 4.68 m (15 ft. 4 ¼ in.); H. 33 cm (13 in.)
Courtesy of the Malloch Rare Book Room of the New York Academy of Medicine Library

The Edwin Smith Papyrus is named after its original owner, an American Egyptologist (1822–1906) who purchased it in Luxor in 1862. At his death it was presented by his daughter to the New-York Historical Society. Loaned to the Brooklyn Museum for display in 1938, it was donated by both of these institutions to the New York Academy of Medicine in 1948.

The papyrus originally comprised twelve sheets glued into a continuous roll; it was cut into separate sheets by Smith. The first sheet, which would have been on the outside of the papyrus when it was rolled, is fragmentary, but the remainder of the document has survived relatively intact. The papyrus is inscribed, in red and black ink, with seventeen columns of text on the recto and five on the verso; the text on the verso is inscribed on the back of columns 17–13. The end of the papyrus is uninscribed on either side, a total of about 27.5 cm (10 ¹³⁄₁₆ in.).

The recto and most of the verso were written by a single scribe; a second hand wrote the last thirteen lines of column 4 and all of column 5 of the verso. The text is in hieratic, the cursive form of Egypt's hieroglyphic script, which is written from right to left in horizontal lines. The form of its signs is that in use at the end of the Second Intermediate Period, about 1650–1550 B.C., when the south of Egypt was governed by the Sixteenth and Seventeenth Dynasties, ruling at Thebes (modern Luxor). The papyrus itself was almost certainly written in Thebes and eventually placed either in a temple library or in the tomb of its last ancient owner. Both the form of its language and mistakes made by the scribe indicate that it is not an original composition but a copy of a document some two to three hundred years older.

The fragmentary first sheet is most likely the original beginning of the papyrus. Its verso may have borne a short title, such as "Beginning of the secret knowledge of a physician," similar to the Ebers Papyrus, another medical document. The seventeen columns of the recto

contain analyses and treatments for forty-eight different types of wounds, beginning with the top of the head and extending to the torso. The scribe ended his copy before finishing the text of the final case, leaving the remainder of the recto blank. The verso contains eight magic spells for use by the physician or his patient and five prescriptions for various ailments. These were probably copied from a source different from that of the recto (undoubtedly so in the case of the last two prescriptions, which were written by a different scribe).

The text of the forty-eight cases on the recto, apparently intended to be a practical guide for the ancient physician in treating wounds of the head or torso, is unlike that of any other medical document that has survived from ancient Egypt. Each case begins with a title, usually written in red ink except where the final words of the previous case were in red. The title begins with the word *sš3w*, translated here as "practices" but meaning more precisely "knowledge gained from practical experience." Following this is advice for the physician in diagnosing the wound and a recommended prognosis. The latter fall into three categories: "an ailment I will handle," characterizing an injury for which a practical remedy existed; "an ailment I will fight with," denoting one whose treatment or outcome was less certain; and "an ailment for which nothing is done," meaning one for which no practical treatment was known. For injuries of the first two types, the recommended treatment then follows.

Twenty-nine of the cases also include one or more explanations of terms used in the diagnosis or treatment to ensure that the attending physician knew exactly what was meant. The first explanation in Case 1, unfortunately damaged, includes a remarkable explanation of the process of diagnosis, defining it as a quantifiable science comparable to that of measuring and tabulating grain. It also contains a rudimentary explanation of the circulatory system, noting its origins in the heart. With two exceptions—the fourth explanation in Case 8 and a magic spell included in the treatment of Case 9—the texts of all forty-eight cases are similarly practical and objective.

The injuries described in all but three of the cases are fractures or flesh wounds caused by external agents, and the patient in every instance is described as a man. Such injuries could be incurred in the course of everyday life or labor in ancient Egypt, which was both perilous and hard, but they could also result from warfare. Indeed, the end of the historical period when the papyrus was copied was marked by skirmishes between the Sixteenth and Seventeenth Dynasties, ruling in Thebes, and the Hyksos (Dynasty 15), which governed the north of Egypt. It is tempting to speculate that the scribe's interest in the text was perhaps prompted by the need to treat wounds resulting from these battles.

The eight magic spells on the verso of the papyrus were mostly intended for use against air-borne pestilence and disease, but they also include one for preventing harm from an accidentally swallowed fly and an interesting spell that apparently was for warding off mental or emotional distress. The latter, like the fourth explanation in Case 8, reveals the causes the Egyptians saw behind unexplained illnesses: "the breath of a god from outside, or a dead man" (Case 8) and the malevolent spirits of those who have died from any cause (Spell 5).

Among the three prescriptions written by the scribe of the recto and of the magic spells is a practical one for menstrual blockage and two for cosmetic purposes. The second scribe added a detailed prescription for an ointment used to combat a head cold as well as for "rejuvenation of the skin and repelling of wrinkles, any age

spots, any sign of old age, and any fever that may be in the body," and another for relieving hemorrhoidal inflammation.

Each column of the papyrus is illustrated and translated below. The translations reflect the original as much as possible, with red and black print corresponding to the red and black ink of the papyrus. Strikeouts in the papyrus are indicated by comparable notations in the translation, and the scribe's secondary insertions by text within angled brackets. Following standard Egyptological convention, square brackets indicate text lost in the papyrus, and parentheses mark modern editorial additions to the body of the text. Titles in SMALL CAPITAL LETTERS are also modern additions. Medical commentary in the footnotes is by David T. Mininberg, M.D.

BIBLIOGRAPHY

J. H. Breasted, *The Edwin Smith Surgical Papyrus*, 2 vols., Oriental Institute Publications 3–4 (Chicago: University of Chicago Press, 1930); H. von Deines et al., *Übersetzung der medizinischen Texte*, 2 vols., Grundriss der Medizin der Alten Ägypter, IV (Berlin: Akademie Verlag, 1958); H. Grapow, *Die medizinischen Texte in hieroglyphischer Umschreibung autographiert*, Grundriss der Medizin der Alten Ägypter, V (Berlin: Akademie Verlag, 1958).

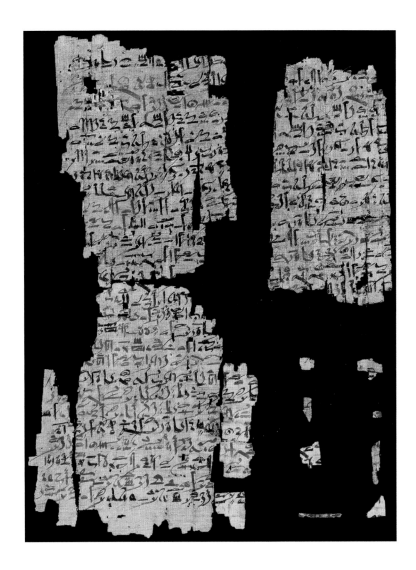

CASE 1. A FLESH WOUND IN THE HEAD (1,1–12)[1]

TITLE
[Practices for a man who suffers from a wound in his head, which has reached to the bone of his skull without gaping.

EXAMINATION AND PROGNOSIS
If you treat a man with a] wound in his head, whose wound's lips [are closed] and not gaping, and [. . .], [then you say about him: "One who has a wound in] his head: an ailment I will handle."

TREATMENT
You have to bandage him with fresh meat the first day and treat him afterward with an oil and [honey] dressing every day until he gets well.

EXPLANATIONS
As for "you treat a man," [it is] taking account of someone [. . . like] taking account of things with a grain measure, treating [being like] one [takes account of] whatever things with a grain measure or takes account of something with the fingers in order to [. . .] them. As for measuring things with a grain measure [. . .], suffering is taken account of in the same way.

Measuring a man's suffering in order to [. . .]. [As for] the heart, there are vessels from it to [every] limb. [As for] that [on] which any lay-priest of Sekhmet and physician puts his hands or his fingers—[on the head, on the back of the] head, on the hands, on the pulse, on the legs—[he] measures the heart. For it is the case that its vessels are in the back of the head and in the pulse, and it is the case that [it speaks] to every vessel and every limb, revealing the measurement of his [. . .]—on the vessels of his head, of the back of his head, of his legs. [. . .] his heart in order to learn the knowledge that comes from it, for [it] reveals its measurement to one who would learn what has happened there.

As for "who suffers from [. . .] his wound," it is to say his wound is small, [not wide], without gaping from one side to the other.

As for "which has reached to [the bone of his skull without] gaping," it is to say there has been gaping by the flesh, while that which [. . .] on the bone of his skull has no gaping from [one side to the other] and is small, not wide.

CASE 2. A GAPING HEAD WOUND (1,12–18)

TITLE

Practices for a [gaping] wound [in his head], which has penetrated to the bone.

EXAMINATION AND PROGNOSIS

If you treat a man for a [gaping wound in] his [head], which has penetrated to the bone, you have to put your hand on him [and you have to] probe his [wound]. If you find his skull [sound], there being [no] violation in it, then you say about [him]: "One who has a gaping [wound] in his head: an ailment I will handle."

TREATMENT

[You] have to [bandage him with fresh meat the first day, and you have to put two lengths of cloth on him and treat him afterward with an oil and honey dressing] every day until he gets well.

EXPLANATIONS

As for "a [gaping] wound [in his head, which has penetrated to the bone," it means . . .] his wound.

As for "two lengths of cloth," [it is] two strips [of cloth, which one puts on the lips of the gaping wound in order to make one side cling to] the other.

As for "without a split or violation [in it," it means . . .].

CASE 3. A HEAD WOUND WITH SKULL DAMAGE (1,18–2,2)[2]

TITLE

[Practices for] a gaping wound in his head, which has penetrated to the bone and violated [his skull.

EXAMINATION AND PROGNOSIS

If you treat a man for a gaping wound in] his [head], which has penetrated to the bone and violated his skull, you have to probe his wound. [Should you] find [him unable to look at his arms and] his chest, and suffering from stiffness in his neck, then you say about him: "One who [has a gaping wound in his head, which has penetrated to the bone and violated] his skull, who suffers from stiffness in his neck: an ailment I will handle."

TREATMENT

After [you stitch him, you have to put] fresh [meat] the first day on his wound. You should not bandage him. He is to be put down [on his bed until the time of his injury passes], and you should treat him afterward with an oil and honey dressing every day until he gets well.

EXPLANATIONS

[As for "a gaping wound in his head, which has penetrated to the bone and violated] his skull, it is a small fracture because of his incurring a fracture like the cracking of a jar [. . .] he has [incurred].

As for "unable to look at his arms and [his] chest," [it means that it is not easy for him when he looks at] his arms and it is not easy for him when he looks at his chest.

As for "suffers from stiffness

NOTES

1. The raw meat prescribed in the treatment contains enzymes that are useful for cleansing a wound. The discussion of the heart and pulse, which seems out of context here, is perhaps the earliest description of the circulatory system. Although the Egyptians' observations about the circulatory system are not completely accurate, the concepts of the heart as the center of the system and of the vessels transporting material from the heart to the rest of the body are essentially correct. The use of the pulse to monitor heart function and abnormalities reflects current medical practice.
2. This deep wound, penetrating to the bone, required suturing to adequately repair it. To bring the edges of wounds together, physicians used linen sutures with bone or copper needles and strips of linen much like today's butterfly bandages. The precise system of wound description and classification insured proper treatment.

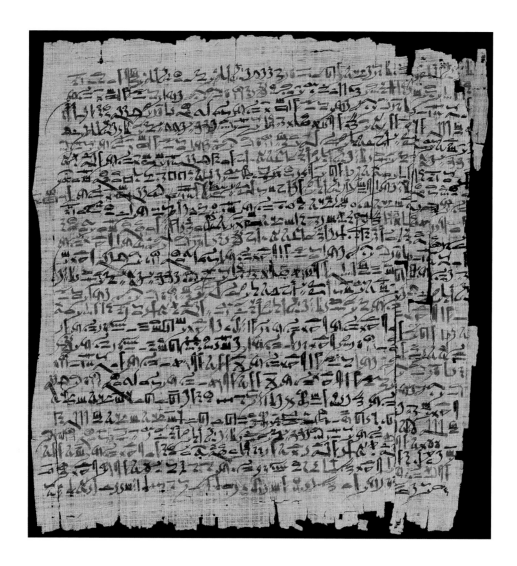

in his neck," it means stiffening from his having previously been injured, this having traveled into his neck so that his neck has to suffer from it.

As for "he is to be put down on his bed," it is putting him on his bed and checking him without making a prescription for him.

CASE 4. A HEAD WOUND WITH DAMAGE TO THE PLATES OF THE SKULL (2,2–11)

TITLE

Practices for a gaping wound in his head, which has penetrated to the bone and split his skull.

EXAMINATION AND PROGNOSIS

If you treat a man for a gaping wound in his head, which has penetrated to the bone and split his skull, you have to probe his wound. Should you find something there uneven under your fingers, should he be very much in pain at it, and should the swelling that is on it be high, while he bleeds from his nostrils and his ears, suffers stiffness in his neck, and is unable to look at his arms and his chest, then you say about him: "One who has a gaping wound in his head, which has penetrated to the bone and split his skull, while he bleeds from his nostrils and his ears and suffers stiffness in his neck: an ailment I will fight with."

TREATMENT

Since you find that man with his skull split, you should not bandage him. He is to be put down on his bed until the time of his injury passes. Sitting is his treatment, with two supports of brick made for him, until you learn that he arrives at a turning point. You have to put oil on his head and soften his neck and shoulders with it. You should do likewise for any man you find with his skull split.

EXPLANATIONS

As for "which has split his skull," it is the pushing away of one plate of his skull from another, while the pieces stay in the flesh of his head and do not fall down.

As for "the swelling on it is high," it means that the bloating that is on that split is great and lifted upward.

As for "you learn that he arrives at a turning point," it is to say you learn that he will die or until he has revived, since it is "an ailment I will fight with."

CASE 5. A HEAD WOUND WITH SKULL FRACTURE (2,11–17)[3]

TITLE

Practices for a gaping wound in his head that has fractured his skull.

EXAMINATION AND PROGNOSIS

If you treat a man for a gaping wound in his head, which has penetrated to the bone and fractured his skull, you have to probe that wound. Should you find that fracture that is in his skull deep and sunken under your fingers, and should the swelling that is on it be high, while he bleeds from his nostrils and his ears, suffers stiffness in his neck, and is unable to look at his shoulders and his chest, then you say about him: "One who has a gaping wound in his head, which has penetrated to the bone and fractured his skull, and who suffers from stiffness in his neck: an ailment for which nothing is done."

TREATMENT

You should not bandage him. He is to be put down on his bed until the time of his injury passes.

EXPLANATION

As for "which has fractured his skull," it is fracturing his skull, with the bones that happen from that fracture sunken to the inside of his skull. The treatise "The Nature of Wounds" has said about it: it is the fracturing of his skull into many pieces, sunken to the inside of his skull.

CASE 6. A HEAD WOUND WITH SKULL FRACTURE EXPOSING THE BRAIN (2,17–3,1)[4]

TITLE

Practices for a gaping wound in his head, which has penetrated to the bone, fractured his skull, and exposed the brain of his skull.

EXAMINATION AND PROGNOSIS

If you treat a man for a gaping wound in his head, which has penetrated to the bone, fractured his skull, and exposed the brain of his skull, you have to probe that wound. Should you find that fracture that is in his skull like those ripples that happen in copper through smelting, with a thing in it that throbs and flutters under your fingers like the weak spot of the crown of a boy before it becomes whole for him—that throbbing and fluttering happens under your fingers since the brain of his skull has become exposed—while he bleeds from his nostrils and suffers stiffness in his neck: an ailment for which nothing is done.

TREATMENT

You should sprinkle that wound of his with oil. You should not bandage him. You should not put dressings on him until you learn that he arrives at a turning point.

EXPLANATIONS

As for "which has fractured his skull and exposed the brain of his skull," it is a big fracture, which is open to the inside of his skull and the membrane that covers his brain; it has to fracture so that it gushes from inside his head.

As for "those ripples that happen in copper through smelting," it is copper that a coppersmith pours

NOTES

3. This case of a depressed skull fracture that obviously involves the nervous system illustrates the physician's recognition of the limits of his abilities, as he offers only supportive care rather than "heroic" measures.

4. Here the wound has penetrated all the way to the surface of the brain. The sulci (grooves on the surface of the brain) are described as being like poured molten copper. There is also a clear understanding of the fontanelle, the gap in the plates of a child's skull that closes by adulthood.

before he has shaped it into something in a mold, its surface being uneven like wrinkles—that is to say, it is like ripples of pus.

CASE 7. A HEAD WOUND DAMAGING THE SKULL'S SUTURES (3,2–4,4)

TITLE
Practices for a gaping wound in his head, which has penetrated to the bone and violated the sutures of his skull.

EXAMINATION AND PROGNOSIS
(If you treat a man for a gaping wound in his head, which has penetrated to the bone and violated the sutures of his skull), you have to probe his wound. Should he be very much in pain at it, then you make him lift his face, since it is too hard for him to open his mouth and his heart is too weary for him to talk. If you notice spittle fallen from his lip but not falling to the ground, and he bleeds from his nostrils and from his ears, and he suffers stiffness in his neck and is unable to look at his shoulders and his chest, then you say about him: "One who has a gaping wound in his head, which has penetrated to the bone and violated the sutures of his skull, the cord of his jaw having contracted, while he bleeds from his nostrils and from his ears, and suffers stiffness in his neck: an ailment I will fight with."

TREATMENT
Since you find that man with the cord of his jaw contracted, you have to have something warm made for him until he gets well. His mouth has to open, and you bandage him with an oil and honey dressing until you learn that he arrives at a turning point.

ALTERNATIVE EXAMINATION AND PROGNOSIS
But if you find that man with a fever from that wound that is in the sutures of his skull, and that man has a toothache from that wound, then you put your hand on him. Should you find his face damp from sweat, the vessels of his neck taut, his face ruddy, and his teeth and back, the smell of the box of his head like the urine of sheep and goats, his mouth clenched, his eyebrows knit, and his face like something crying, then you say about him: "One who has a gaping wound in his head, which has penetrated to the bone and violated the sutures of his skull, who has a toothache, whose mouth is clenched, who suffers from stiffness in his neck: an ailment for which nothing is done."

ALTERNATIVE TREATMENT
But if you find that man whitened, having previously exhibited weakness, you have to have a chisel of wood covered with cloth made for him and applied to his mouth. You have to have a soup of carob beans made for him. Sitting between two supports of brick is his treatment, until you learn that he arrives at a turning point.

EXPLANATIONS
As for "violated the sutures of (his skull)," it is what is between one plate of his skull and another. The sutures will be leathery.

As for "the cords of his jaw contracted," it is stiffening because of it by the vessels of the end of his ramus, which are fastened in his temporal bone—that is the end of his mandible—without moving back and forth, while opening his mouth is not easy for him because of his injury.

As for "the cord of his jaw," it is the vessels that bind the ends of his mandible, like saying the cord of a thing, consisting of a string.

As for "his face damp from sweat," it means that his head is sweaty a little, like the dampness of something.

As for "the vessels of his neck taut," it means that the vessels of his neck are taut and stiff from his injury.

As for "his face ruddy," it means that the color of his face is red, like the color of red fruit.

As for "the smell of the box of his head like the urine of sheep and goats,"

RECTO, COLUMN 4

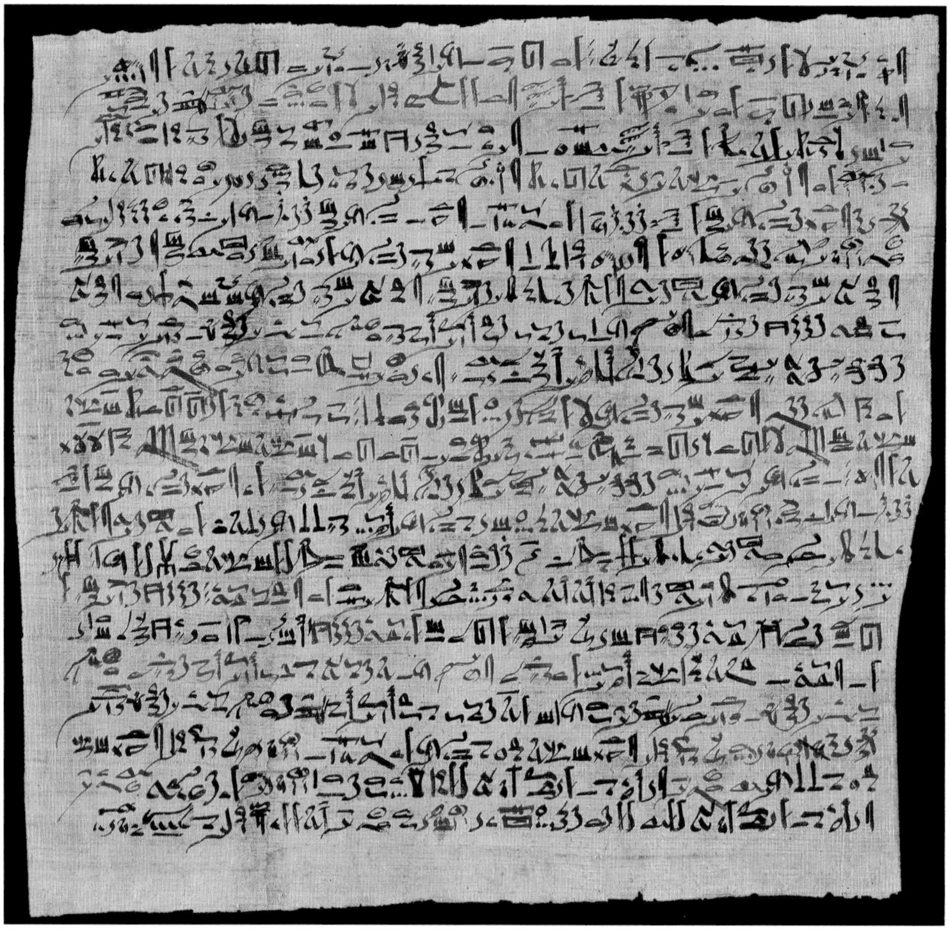

it means that the smell of his forehead is like the urine of sheep and goats.

As for "the box of his head," it is the middle of his forehead at the area of his brain: it is similar to a box.

As for "his mouth clenched, his eyebrows knit, and his face like something crying," it means that he does not open his mouth to speak, while his eyebrows are contracted and move upward or downward like one who is blinking when his face is crying.

As for "whitened, having previously exhibited weakness," it is the whitening of one who is in danger—as one who meets a poisonous snake—because of weakness.

CASE 8. A HIDDEN SKULL FRACTURE (4,5–18)[5]

TITLE
Practices for a fracture in his skull under the skin of his head.

EXAMINATION AND PROGNOSIS
If you treat a man for a fracture of his skull under the skin of his head, there being nothing on the surface, you have to probe his wound. Should you find a swelling risen above that fracture that is in his skull, while his eye is askew from it on the side with that fracture that is in his skull, and he walks shuffling with his foot on the side with that fracture that is in his skull, you should distinguish him from one afflicted because of something that has entered from the outside, being one in whose shoulder the head of the bone is not loosened and one whose fingernail cannot touch the palm of his hand, while he bleeds from his nostrils and from his ears and suffers stiffness in his neck: an ailment for which nothing is done.

TREATMENT
His treatment is sitting until he feels better or until you learn that he arrives at a turning point. Since you find that smash that is in his skull like those ripples that happen in copper through smelting, with a thing in it that throbs and flutters under your fingers like the weak spot of the crown of a boy before it becomes whole—that throbbing and fluttering happens under your fingers once the brain of his skull becomes exposed—while he bleeds from his nostrils and from his ears and suffers stiffness in his neck, it is an ailment for which nothing is done.

EXPLANATIONS
As for "a fracture of his skull under the skin of his head, there being no wound on him," it is a fracture of the plate of his skull, while the flesh that is on his head is sound.

As for "he walks shuffling with his foot," it refers to his walking with his foot inert, and it is not easy for him to walk, it being weak and dangling, with the tips of his toes bent toward his instep and seeking the ground when they walk: it means he shuffles because of it.

As for "one afflicted because of something that has entered from the outside" in his side that has this injury, it is the penetration of something that enters from outside into his side that has this injury.

As for "something that has entered from the outside," it is the breath of a god from outside, or a dead man, making entry, not something his body has created.

As for "one in whose shoulder the head of the bone is not loosened and one whose fingernail cannot touch the palm of his hand," it refers (to) the head of the bone of his shoulder not being usable for him and his fingernail not touching the palm ⟨of⟩ his hand.

CASE 9. A FOREHEAD WOUND WITH SKULL FRACTURE (4,19–5,5)[6]

TITLE
Practices for a wound in the front of his face, which has fractured the shell of his skull.

EXAMINATION AND TREATMENT
If you treat a man for a wound in the front of his face, which has fractured the shell of his skull, you have to make him the egg of an ostrich, ground with oil, and put in the mouth of his wound. Afterward, you have to make him the egg of an ostrich, ground and made into a powder: that is what dries the wound. You have to put for him a cloth of a physician's outfit on it.

NOTES
5. As the skull is fractured without a visible external wound, the physician postulates intrusion by an external (supernatural) force. The description of symptoms on the same side as the fracture suggests that the actual injury to the brain was on the other side, a result of pressure from the initial trauma (known as the contra-coup effect).
6. The explanation of this case refers to "cloth of the physician's outfit" (equipment) as linen obtained from the bandager (embalmer), suggesting that there was significant contact between these two professional groups.

You have to uncover it on the 3rd day: you will find × ⟨it has knit⟩ the shell, the color being like the egg of an ostrich.

What is said as magic over this prescription: "The enemy in the wound has been driven off; the conspiracy in the blood has been made to tremble; the vulture of every side has been given to the mouth of the effective goddess. This temple will not deteriorate; there is no crocodile or poison therein. For I am in the effective goddess's protection: Osiris's son is rescued."

Afterward, you have to cool for him the fruit of figs, oil, and honey, cooked, cooled, and given to him.

EXPLANATION

As for "a cloth of a physician's outfit," it is the strip of cloth that is used by the bandager: he should put it on the prescription that is on the wound that is in the front of his face.

CASE 10. A WOUND IN THE EYEBROW (5,5–9)

TITLE

Practices for a wound in the tip of his eyebrow.

EXAMINATION AND PROGNOSIS

If you treat a man for a wound in the tip of his eyebrow, which has penetrated to the bone, you have to probe his wound and fasten its gap for him with thread. Then you say about him: "A wound in his eyebrow: an ailment I will handle."

TREATMENT

After you sew him, (you have to bandage him) with fresh meat the first day. If you find this wound with its sewing slipped, you have to fasten it for him with two lengths of cloth. You should treat him with oil and honey every day until he gets well.

EXPLANATION

As for "two lengths of cloth," they are two strips of cloth. They are put on the lips of a gaping wound in order to make one adhere to the other.

CASE 11. A FRACTURE OF THE NASAL CARTILAGE (5,10–15)

TITLE

Practices for a fracture in the pillar of his nose.

EXAMINATION AND PROGNOSIS

If you treat a man for a fracture in the pillar of his nose, and his nose is flattened and his face is flattened out, while the swelling that is on it is high, and he has bled from his nostrils, then you say about him: "One who has a fracture in the pillar of his nose: an ailment I will handle."

TREATMENT

You have to wipe it for him with two plugs of cloth. You have to push two plugs of cloth wet with oil inside his nostrils. You have to put him on his bed in order to reduce his swelling. You have to set for him stiff rolls of cloth so that his nose is restricted from moving, and treat him afterward with an oil and honey dressing every day until he gets well.

EXPLANATIONS

As for "the pillar of his nose," it is the bridge and side of his nose, inside his nose in the middle of his nostrils. As for "his nostrils," they are the two sides of his nose, penetrating to his cheek, starting at the end of his nose and exiting the top of his nose.

CASE 12. A FRACTURE OF THE NASAL BONE (5,16–6,3)

TITLE

Practices for a fracture in the chamber of his nose.

EXAMINATION AND PROGNOSIS

If you treat a man for a fracture in the chamber of his nose and you find his nose crooked and his face flattened, while the swelling that is on it is high, then you say about him: "One who has a fracture in the chamber of his nose: an ailment I will handle."

TREATMENT

Set it back in its proper place. Wipe for him the inside of his nostrils with two strips of cloth until every eel of blood that is knotted inside his nostrils comes out. Afterward, you have to push two plugs of cloth wet with oil into his nostrils. You have to set for him two stiff rolls of cloth bandaged on it and treat ⟨him⟩ with an oil and honey dressing every day until he gets well.

EXPLANATIONS

As for "a fracture in the chamber of his nose," it is the middle part of his nose down to where it ends between his eyebrows.

As for "his nose crooked and his face flattened," it means that his nose is awry and very swollen all over, and his cheeks likewise, so his face is flattened out from it and is not in its right form, because

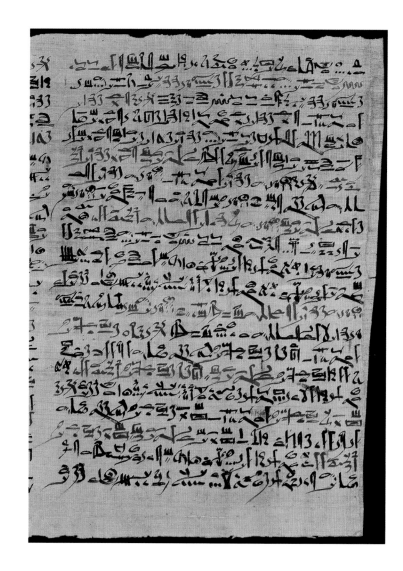

every sinus is distorted with swelling, so his face looks flattened from it.

As for "every eel of blood that is knotted inside his nostrils," it is the coagulated blood inside his nostrils, similar to the eel that exists in the water.

CASE 13. A FRACTURE OF ONE SIDE OF THE NOSE (6,4–7)

TITLE
Practices for a fracture in his nose.

EXAMINATION AND PROGNOSIS
If you treat a man for a fracture in his nose, you have to put your hand on his nose in the area of that fracture. Should it wiggle under your fingers, while he also bleeds from his nostril and from his ear near that fracture, and it is hard for him to open his mouth from it, and he is dazed, then you say about him: "One who has a fracture in his nose: an ailment for which nothing is done."

CASE 14. A FLESH WOUND IN THE NOSE (6,7–14)

TITLE
Practices for a wound in his nose.

EXAMINATION AND PROGNOSIS
If you treat a man for a wound in his nostril, which is obstructive, and if you find the lips of that wound shifted from each other, you have to fasten that wound for him with stitches. Then you say about him: "One who has a wound in his nose, which is obstructive: an ailment I will handle."

TREATMENT
You have to make for him two swabs of cloth. You have to wipe every eel of blood that is knotted inside his nostril. You have to bandage him with fresh meat the first day. If

his stitches loosen after you have taken away the fresh meat from it, you have to bandage him with an oil and honey dressing every day until he gets well.

EXPLANATION
As for "a wound in his nostril, which is obstructive," it means that the lips of his wound are flabby and open to the inside of his nose as well, the flabbiness forming an obstruction.

CASE 15. A CHEEK WOUND (6,14–17)

TITLE
Practices for a perforation in his cheek.

EXAMINATION AND PROGNOSIS
If you treat a man for a perforation in his cheek and you find a swelling on his cheek risen, black, and gone off, then you say about him: "One who has a perforation in his cheek: an ailment I will handle."

TREATMENT
You have to bandage him with alum and treat him afterward with oil and honey every day until he gets well.

CASE 16. A SPLIT CHEEK (6,17–21)

TITLE
Practices for a split in his cheek.

EXAMINATION AND PROGNOSIS
If you treat a man for a split in his cheek and you find a swelling risen and red over that split, then you say about him: "One who has a split in his cheek: an ailment I will handle."

TREATMENT
You have to bandage him with fresh meat the first day. His treatment is to sit in order to reduce his swelling. You should treat him afterward with an oil and honey dressing every day until he gets well.

CASE 17. A FRACTURED CHEEKBONE (7,1–7)

TITLE
Practices for a fracture in his cheek.

EXAMINATION AND PROGNOSIS
If you treat a man for a fracture in his cheek, you have to put your hand on his cheek in the area of that fracture. Should it wiggle under your fingers, while he is bleeding from his nostril and from his ear on his side that has that blow, and he also is bleeding from his mouth and it is hard to open his mouth from it, then you say about him: "One who has a fracture in his cheek, who bleeds from his nose, from his ear, and from his cheek, and is dazed: an ailment for which nothing is done."

TREATMENT
You have to bandage with fresh meat the first day. He should be forced to sit in order to reduce his swelling, and treat him afterward with an oil and honey dressing every day until he gets well.

CASE 18. A FLESH WOUND OF THE TEMPLE (7,7–14)

TITLE
Practices for a wound in his temple.

EXAMINATION AND PROGNOSIS
If you treat a man for a wound in his temple that has no gaping, although that wound has penetrated to the bone, you have to probe his wound. Should you find his temple sound, with no split, perforation, or fracture in it, then you say about him: "One who has a wound in his temple: an ailment I will handle."

TREATMENT
You have to bandage him with fresh meat the first day and treat afterward with oil and honey every day until he gets well.

EXPLANATIONS
As for "a wound that ⟨has⟩ no gaping, although it has penetrated to the bone," it means that the wound that has

reached the bone is little and no gaping has developed in it: it refers to a narrow one, his wound having no ~~his~~ lips.

As for "his temple," it is what is between the end of his eye and the auricle of his ear at the top of his mandible.

CASE 19. A MINOR PERFORATION OF THE TEMPLE (7,14–20)

TITLE
Practices for a perforation in his temple.

EXAMINATION AND PROGNOSIS
If you treat a man for a perforation in his temple, with a wound on it, you have to observe that wound. Should you say to him: "Look at your shoulders," and it is hard for him to do, and he can only turn his neck a little, and his eye is bloodshot on his side that has that blow, then you say about him: "One who has a perforation in his temple and is suffering from stiffness in his neck: an ailment I will handle."

TREATMENT
You have to put him on his bed until the time of his injury has passed and treat with an oil and honey dressing every day until he gets well.

EXPLANATION
As for "his eye is bloodshot," it means that the color of his eyes is red, like the color of the *š3s* plant. The treatise of "Skill of the Embalmer" says about it that his eyes are red and sore, like an overtired eye.

CASE 20. A SERIOUS PERFORATION OF THE TEMPLE (7,20–8,5)

TITLE
Practices for a wound in his temple, which has penetrated to the bone and perforated his temple.

EXAMINATION AND PROGNOSIS
If you treat a man for a wound in his temple, which has penetrated to the bone and perforated his temple, while his two eyes are bloodshot and he bleeds a little from his nostrils, and if you put your fingers on the mouth of

that wound and he is very much in pain at it, and if you ask what he suffers from and he does not speak to you, and many tears have fallen from his eyes and he has to take his hand to his face many times, wiping his eyes with the back of his hand as a boy does, and he does not know what he does, then you say about him: "One who has a wound in his temple, which has penetrated to the bone and perforated his temple, who bleeds from his nostrils, suffers stiffness in his neck, and is dazed: an ailment I will handle."

TREATMENT

Since you find that man dazed, he should be forced to sit, his head softened with oil and congealed oil poured into his ears.

CASE 21. A SPLIT TEMPLE (8,6–9)

TITLE

Practices for a split in his temple.

EXAMINATION AND PROGNOSIS

If you treat a man for a split in his temple and you find a swelling risen over that split, while he is bleeding from his one nostril and ear where that split is, and it is hard for him to hear talking from it, then you say about him: "One who has a split in his temple, bleeding from his nostril and his ear from that blow: an ailment I will fight with."

TREATMENT

You have to put him on his bed until you learn that he arrives at a turning point.

CASE 22. FRACTURE OF THE TEMPORAL BONE (8,9–17)

TITLE

Practices for a fracture in his temple.

EXAMINATION AND PROGNOSIS

If you treat a man for a fracture in his temple, you have to put your finger on his chin and your finger on the end of his ramus. Blood will fall from his nostrils and the interior of his ears from that fracture. Wipe for him with a plug of cloth until you see its chips inside his ears. If you have called to him and he is dazed and does not speak, then you say about him: "One who has a fracture in his temple, who

bleeds from his nostrils and his ears, is dazed, and suffers stiffness in his neck: an ailment for which nothing is done."

EXPLANATIONS

As for "the end of his ramus," it is the end of his jawbone. The ramus ends in his temple, like the claw of a plover taking hold of something.

As for "you see its chips inside his ears," it means that chips of bone keep coming to adhere to the plug inserted to wipe inside his ears.

As for "he is dazed," it means that he is continually still and in depression, without speaking, like one who has paralysis because of something that will has entered from outside.

CASE 23. A TORN EAR (8,18–24)

TITLE

Practices for a wound in his ear.

EXAMINATION AND PROGNOSIS

If you treat a man for a wound in his ear that has cut down to the opening of its body, while there is still something of the lower part of his ear remaining in the body, you have to fasten it for him with stitching behind the hollow of his ear. Then you say about him: "One who has a wound in his ear that has cut down to the opening of its body: an ailment I will handle."

TREATMENT

If you find that wound with its stitching slipped but still fixed in the lips of his wound, you have to make for him stiff rolls of cloth and apply them to the back of his ear. You should treat him afterward with an oil and honey dressing every day until he gets well.

CASE 24. A FRACTURED JAWBONE (8,24–9,2)

TITLE

Practices for a crack in his jaw.

EXAMINATION AND PROGNOSIS

If you treat a man for a crack in his jaw, you have to put your hand on him. Should you find that crack has wiggled under your fingers, then you say about him:

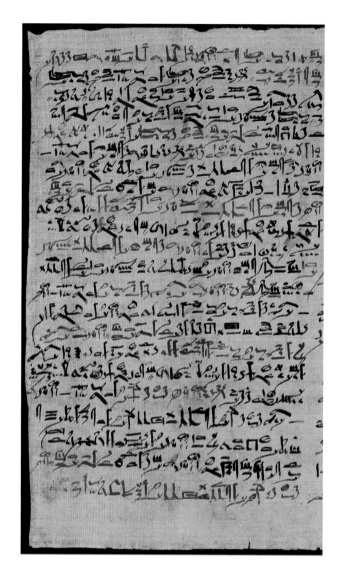

"One who has a crack in his jaw, a wound having erupted over it but stopped oozing, and he has a fever from it: an ailment for which nothing is done."

CASE 25. A DISLOCATED JAWBONE (9,2–6)[7]

TITLE
Practices for a dislocation in his jaw.

EXAMINATION AND PROGNOSIS
If you treat a man with a dislocation in his jaw, and you find his mouth open and unable to close, you have to put your thumb under the end of the rami of the jaw inside his mouth, with your two forefingers under his chin. Then you push them into their place. Then you say about him: "One who has a dislocation in his jaw: an ailment I will handle."

TREATMENT
You have to bandage him with alum and honey every day until he gets well.

CASE 26. A LIP WOUND (9,6–13)

TITLE
Practices for a wound in his lip.

EXAMINATION AND PROGNOSIS
If you treat a man for a wound in his lip obstructing the inside of his mouth, you have to treat his wound up to the pillar of his nose; you have to fasten that wound with stitches. Then you say about him: "One who has a wound in his lip obstructing the inside of his mouth: an ailment I will handle."

TREATMENT
After you stitch him you have to bandage him with fresh meat the first day and treat ⟨him⟩ afterward with oil and honey every day until he gets well.

EXPLANATION
As for "a wound in his lip obstructing the inside of his mouth," it means that the lips of his wound are flabby and open to the inside of his mouth, the flabbiness referring to an obstruction.

CASE 27. A WOUND IN THE CHIN (9,13–18)

TITLE
Practices for a gaping wound in his chin.

EXAMINATION AND PROGNOSIS
If you treat a man for a gaping wound in his chin, which has penetrated to the bone, you have to probe his wound. If you find his bone sound, with no split or perforation in it, then you say about him: "One who has a gaping wound in his chin, which has penetrated to the bone: an ailment I will handle."

TREATMENT
You have to put two strips of cloth on that gash for him. You have to bandage him with fresh meat the first day and treat him afterward with an oil and honey dressing every day until he gets well.

CASE 28. A THROAT WOUND (9,18–10,3)

TITLE
Practices for a wound in his throat.

EXAMINATION AND PROGNOSIS
If you treat a man for a gaping wound in his neck, obstructing his windpipe so that if he drinks water he has to choke and it comes out of the mouth of his wound, and it is enflamed, and he gets a high fever from it, you have to fasten that wound with stitching. Then you say about him: "One who has a wound in his foreneck, obstructing his windpipe: an ailment I will fight with."

NOTE
7. This treatment for the dislocated jaw is in essence the same maneuver that a modern surgeon would employ, although presumably with better analgesia (pain relief).

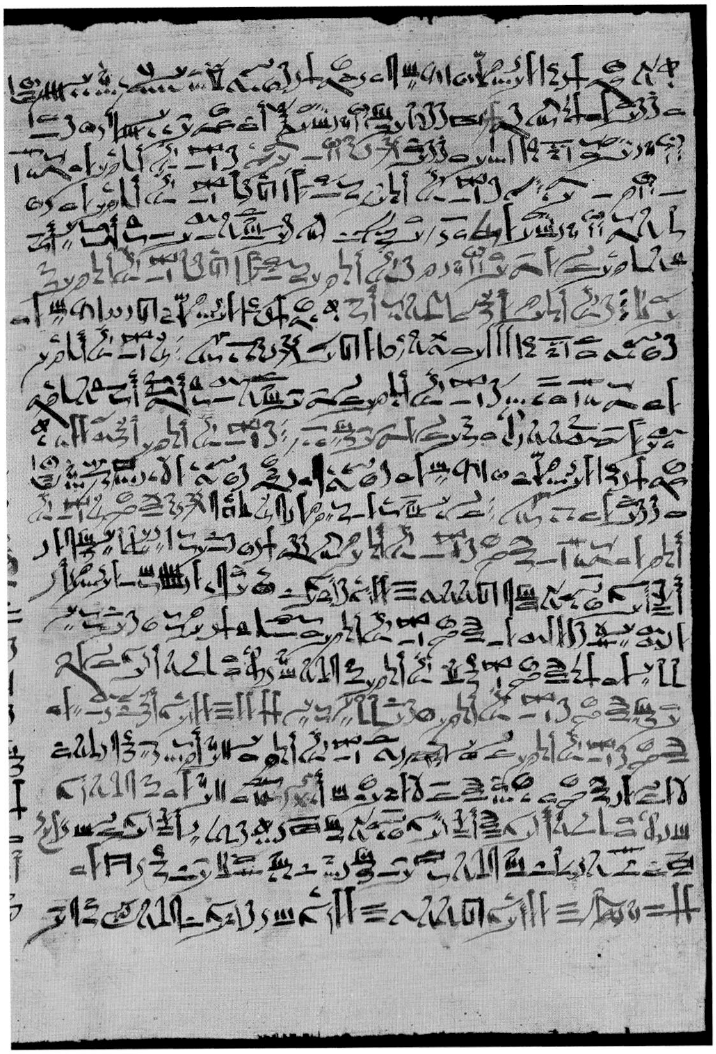

TREATMENT

You have to bandage him with fresh meat the first day and treat him afterward with an oil and honey dressing every day until he gets well. But if you find ⟨him⟩ becoming feverish from that wound, you have to put for him dry fibers on the mouth of his wound, and he is to be put down on his bed until he gets well.

CASE 29. A NECK WOUND (10,3–8)

TITLE

Practices for a gaping wound in a vertebra of his neck.

EXAMINATION AND PROGNOSIS

If you treat a man for a gaping wound in a vertebra of his neck, which has penetrated to the bone and violated a vertebra of his neck, and if you probe that wound and he is very much in pain at it and cannot look at his shoulders and his middle, then you say about him: "One who has a wound in his neck, which has penetrated to the bone and violated a vertebra of his neck, and who suffers from stiffness in his neck: an ailment I will fight with."

TREATMENT

You have to bandage him with fresh meat the first day. Afterward, put (him) down on his bed until the time of his injury passes.

CASE 30. A SPRAINED NECK (10,8–12)

TITLE

Practices for a sprain in a vertebra of his neck.

EXAMINATION AND PROGNOSIS

If you treat a man for a sprain in a vertebra of his neck and you say to him "Look at your shoulders and your middle" and when he does so it is hard for him to look because of it, then you say about him: "One who has a sprain in a vertebra of his neck: an ailment I will handle."

TREATMENT

You have to bandage him with fresh meat the first day. Afterward, you should treat with alum and honey every day until he gets better.

EXPLANATION

As for "a sprain," it refers to a pulling apart by two members while each is still in place.

CASE 31. A DISLOCATED NECK VERTEBRA (10,12–22)[8]

TITLE

Practices for a dislocation in a vertebra of his neck.

EXAMINATION AND PROGNOSIS

If you treat a man for a dislocation in a vertebra of his neck, and you find him unaware of his arms and his legs from it, and his penis is stiff from it, while urine falls from his penis without him knowing it, and he has become gaseous, and his eyes are bloodshot, it is the shift of a vertebra of his neck, which reaches to his spine, that causes him to be unaware of his arms and his legs; and when the vertebra of his neck is dislocated, the result is erection of his penis. Then you say about him: "One who has a dislocation in a vertebra of his neck, who is unaware of his legs and his arms, and whose urine is inert: an ailment for which nothing is done."

EXPLANATIONS

As for "a dislocation in a vertebra of his neck," it refers to the separation of a vertebra of his neck from its companion, the flesh that is on it being sound, as a thing that keeps in contact at the wrenching of one thing from its companion is said to have become dislocated.

As for "the result is erection of his penis," his penis is continually stiff, with a discharge at the end of his penis. It is to say, ⟨it⟩ stays on guard and cannot droop down nor can it rise up.

As for "whose urine is inert," it means that urine continually falls from his penis and does not build up for him.

NOTE

8. The physician describes the visible dislocated vertebra without appreciating the underlying injury to the spinal cord. Careful reading of the symptom complex, however, vividly documents the paraplegia that would be the diagnosis of a modern physician.

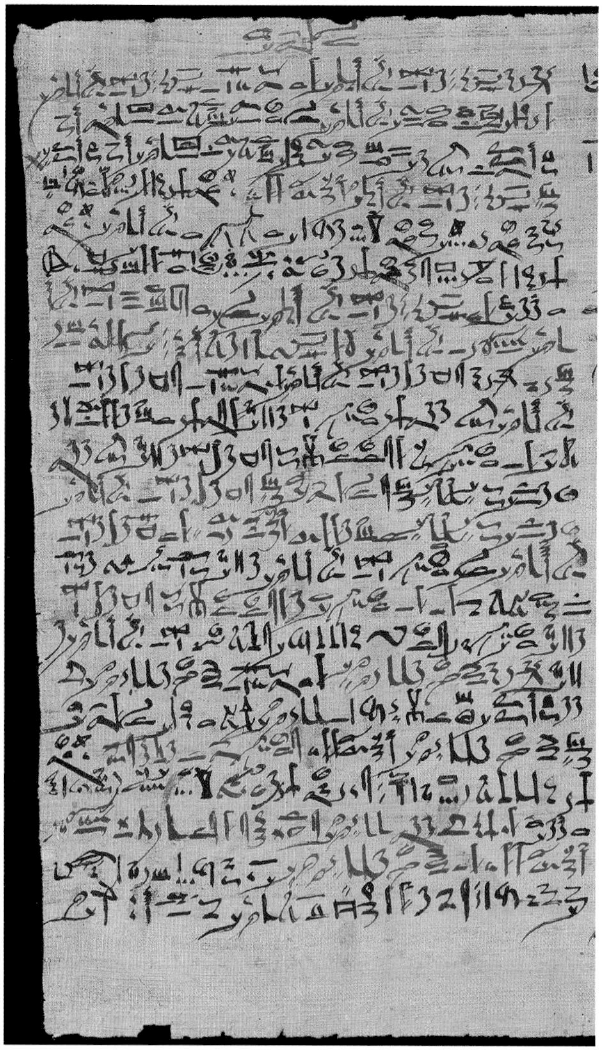

⟨then you say about him:⟩

CASE 32. A SHIFTED NECK VERTEBRA (11,1–9)

TITLE
Practices for a settling in a vertebra of his neck.

EXAMINATION AND PROGNOSIS
If you treat a man for a settling in a vertebra of his neck, and his face is fixed and he cannot turn his neck, you have to say to him: "Look at your breast and your shoulders," and it is impossible for him to turn his face to look at his breast and his shoulders, × "One who has a settling in a vertebra of his neck: an ailment I will handle."

TREATMENT
You have to bandage him with fresh meat the first day. You have to loosen his bandages and you have to put oil on him to run down his neck. You have to bandage him with alum and treat him afterward with honey every day. He should be forced to sit until he gets well.

EXPLANATION
As for "a settling in a vertebra of his neck," it refers to his neck sinking toward the inside of his neck, like a foot sinks in soil. It is a depression downward.

CASE 33. A SHIFTED NECK VERTEBRA (11,9–17)

TITLE
Practices for a contusion in a vertebra of his neck.

EXAMINATION AND PROGNOSIS
If you treat a man for a contusion in a vertebra of his neck and you find him with the vertebra falling into its neighbor, while he is dazed and cannot speak—his falling upside down is what causes a vertebra to contuse its neighbor— and you find he has lost feeling in his arms and his legs

from it, then you say about him: "One who has a contusion in a vertebra of his neck and has lost feeling in his arms and his legs, and is dazed: an ailment for which nothing is done."

EXPLANATIONS
As for "a contusion in a vertebra of his neck," it refers ⟨to⟩ a vertebra of his neck falling into its neighbor, one entering into the other, without moving in or out.

As for "his falling upside down is what causes a vertebra to contuse its neighbor," it means that he falls upside down on his head, so that a vertebra of his neck slots into its neighbor.

CASE 34. A DISLOCATED COLLARBONE (11,17–12,2)[9]

TITLE
Practices for a dislocation in his collarbone.

EXAMINATION AND PROGNOSIS
If you treat a man for a dislocation in his collarbone, whose shoulders are found drooping while the head of his collarbone is facing toward his face, then you say about him: "One who has a dislocation in his collarbone: an ailment I will handle."

TREATMENT
Make it fall back into its place. You have to bandage him with stiff rolls of cloth and treat him afterward with oil and honey every day until he gets well. And if you find his collarbone broken, its surface obstructed on the inside, (it is also) "an ailment I will handle."

EXPLANATION
As for "a dislocation in his collarbone," it means that the heads of his clavicles are twisted so that the heads rest in the upper bone of his chest, penetrating to his throat,

NOTE
9. The dislocation of the clavicle (collarbone) is treated here much the same way it would be by a modern physician.

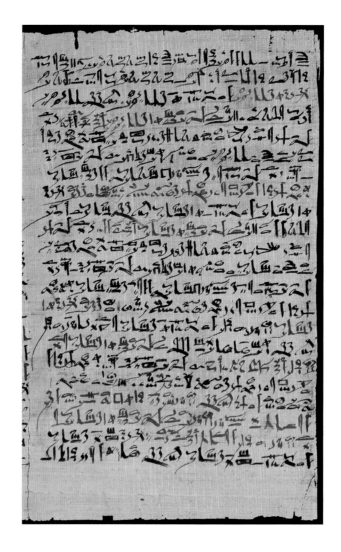

while the flesh of his collarbone area is still on it. It is the flesh that exists on his neck area, with 2 vessels under it, one on the right and the left of his neck area: they give (blood) to his lungs.

CASE 35. A BROKEN COLLARBONE (12,2–8)

TITLE
Practices for a break in his collarbone.

EXAMINATION AND PROGNOSIS
If you treat a man for a break in his collarbone and you find his collarbone shortened and out of alignment with respect to its companion, then you say about him: "One who has a break in his collarbone: an ailment for which nothing is done I will handle."

TREATMENT
Then you lay him out, with something folded between his shoulder blades. You have to pull his shoulders to lengthen his collarbone, until that break falls into its place. Then you make him two strips of cloth. Then you put one of them inside his upper arm and the other below his upper arm. You have to bandage him with alum and treat him afterward with honey every day until he gets well.

CASE 36. A BROKEN UPPER ARM (12,8–14)

TITLE
Practices for a break in his upper arm.

EXAMINATION AND PROGNOSIS
If you treat a man for a break in his upper arm and you find his upper arm dangling away from him and out of alignment with respect to its companion, then you say about him: "One who has a break in his upper arm: an ailment I will handle."

TREATMENT
Then you lay him out, with something folded between his

shoulder blades. You have to pull his arms to lengthen his upper arms, until that break falls into its place. Then you make him two strips of cloth. Then you put one of them inside his upper arm and the other below his upper arm. You have to bandage him with alum and treat him afterward (with) honey every day until he gets well.

CASE 37. A BROKEN UPPER ARM WITH A WOUND (12,14–21)

TITLE
Practices for a break in his upper arm with a wound on it.

EXAMINATION AND PROGNOSIS
If you treat a man for a break in his upper arm, fractured with a wound on it, and you find that break wiggling under your fingers, then you say about him: "One who has a break in his upper arm, fractured with a wound on it: an ailment I will fight with."

TREATMENT
Then you make him two strips of cloth. You have to bandage him with alum and treat him with an oil and honey dressing until you learn that he arrives at a turning point. But if you find that wound that is on the break with blood coming out of it and obstructed on the inside of his wound, then you say about him: "One who has a break in his upper arm with an obstructed wound on it: an ailment for which nothing is done."

CASE 38. A FRACTURED UPPER ARM (12,21–13,2)

TITLE
Practices for a split in his upper arm.

EXAMINATION AND PROGNOSIS
If you treat a man for a split in his upper arm and you find a swelling risen on the back of

that split that is in his upper arm, then you say about him: "One who has a split in his upper arm: an ailment I will handle."

TREATMENT

You have to bandage him with alum and treat him afterward (with) honey every day until he gets well.

CASE 39. A CHEST INFECTION (13,3–12)[10]

TITLE
Practices for an eruption with flattened head in his chest.

EXAMINATION AND PROGNOSIS
If you treat a man for an eruption with flattened head in his chest and you find risings having formed with pus on his chest, making a rash, while there is much warmth there and your hand finds it, then you say about him: "One who has an eruption with flattened head in his chest, ~~they~~ it having made openings of pus: an ailment I will handle."

TREATMENT
You have to sear him on his chest, on that eruption that is on his chest, and treat him with a wound treatment. You should not wait for it to open by itself there: it is not good for his wound. Every wound that occurs in his chest dries out once it opens by itself.

EXPLANATION
As for "an eruption with flattened head in his chest," it means that things are continually swollen and spread out on his chest because of his injury, having made pus and something red on his chest. That is to say, it is like things that have been scratched and create pus.

NOTE
10. This superficial abscess is treated by incision and drainage, similar to what a modern surgeon would do. The "searing" was most probably done with a heated metal rod, the heat from which would control any bleeding, analogous to modern cautery.

CASE 40. A CHEST WOUND (13,12–17)

TITLE
Practices for a wound in his chest.

EXAMINATION AND PROGNOSIS
If you treat a man for a wound in his chest, penetrating to the bone and violating his breastbone, and you touch his breastbone with your fingers and he is very much in pain at it, then you say about him: "One who has a wound in his chest, penetrating to the bone and violating his breastbone: an ailment I will handle."

TREATMENT
You have to bandage him with fresh meat the first day and treat him afterward (with) an oil and honey dressing every day until he gets well.

EXPLANATION
As for "his breastbone," (it is) the upper head of his chest, being like what comes from a hedgehog.

CASE 41. AN INFECTED CHEST WOUND (13,18–14,16)

TITLE
Practices for a wound-infection in his chest.

EXAMINATION AND PROGNOSIS
If you treat a man for a wound-infection in his chest when that wound is inflamed, with a concentration of warmth spewing from the mouth of that wound to your hand, and the lips of that wound are ruddy, and when that man is feverish from it, his flesh does not accept a bandage, and that wound does not acquire a margin of (new) skin, while the crust that is in the mouth of that wound is watery and feverish and the drops

that fall from it are clear, then you say about him: "One who has a wound-infection in his chest, which is inflamed, and he is feverish from it: an ailment I will handle."

TREATMENT

You have to make him a cool medium for drawing the warmth from the mouth of the wound: willow and sidder leaves and *qzntj* mineral, put on it; (or) date palm leaves, gall, grass, and *qzntj* mineral, put on it. You have to make him a medium for drying out the wound: powder of malachite, *wšbt* mineral, faience, and fat, ground and bandaged on it; (or) Delta salt and ibex fat, ground and bandaged on it. You (also) have to make him a powder of poppy seeds, flax seeds, cuttlebone, colocynth, and sycamore leaves, ground and bandaged on it. If the same happens to any limb, you should give it according to these practices.

EXPLANATIONS

As for "a wound-infection in his chest, which is inflamed," it means that that wound that is on his chest is continually agape, without closing over, high heat coming out of it, its lips red and its mouth open; and the treatise "The Nature of Wounds" has said about it that it means that it is continually swollen very much. The high temperature is called inflammation.

As for "a concentration of warmth" in his wound, it means that warmth is concentrated around the entire inside of his wound.

As for "its lips are ruddy," it means that its lips are red like the color of red ocher.

As for "his flesh does not accept a bandage," it means that his flesh does not accept a prescription because of the heat that is on his chest.

And as for "warmth spewing from the mouth of that wound to your hand," warmth comes from the mouth of his wound to your hand, as something that comes out and down is said to spew.

CASE 42. A PULLED RIB (14,16–22)

TITLE

Practices for a pull in the ribs of his chest.

EXAMINATION AND PROGNOSIS

If you treat someone suffering from the ribs of his chest, and there is no dislocation or break, yet that man is suffering and in very much pain, then you say about him: "One who has a pull in the ribs of his chest: an ailment I will handle."

TREATMENT

You have to bandage him with alum and treat him afterward (with) honey every day until he gets well.

EXPLANATION

As for "the ribs of his chest," they are the bones of his chest, which are pointed like what comes from the shoot of a thorn.

CASE 43. A DISLOCATED RIB (14,22–15,6)

TITLE

Practices for a dislocation of the ribs of his chest.

EXAMINATION AND PROGNOSIS

If you treat a man for a dislocation of the ribs of his chest and you find the ribs of his chest mounded

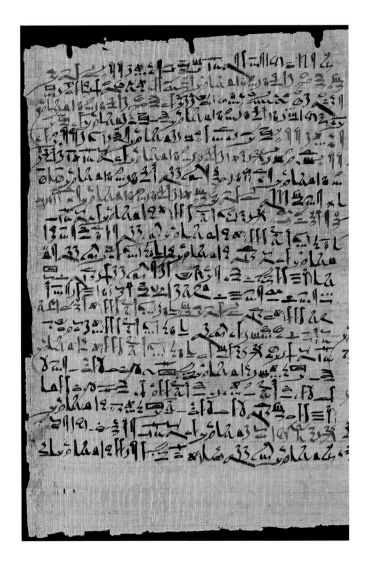

and their head ruddy, while that man suffers from swelling in his sides, then you say about him: "One who has a dislocation in the ribs of his chest: an ailment I will handle."

TREATMENT
You have to bandage him with alum and treat him afterward (with) honey every day until he gets well.

EXPLANATION
As for "a dislocation in the ribs of his chest," it is the loosening of the head of the ribs of his chest, which are normally fixed in his chest.

As for "he suffers from swelling in his sides," it means that he suffers from their pushing in his chest, so that there is swelling in his sides.

As for "his sides," they are his loins.

CASE 44. A BROKEN RIB (15,6–9)

TITLE
Practices for a break in the ribs of his chest.

EXAMINATION AND PROGNOSIS
If you treat a man for a break in the ribs of his chest and the fracture has a wound on it, and you find the ribs of his chest wiggling under your fingers, then you say about him: "One who has a break in the ribs of his chest and a fracture with a wound on it: an ailment for which nothing is done."

CASE 45. CHEST TUMORS (15,9–19)[11]

TITLE
Practices for ball-like tumors on his chest.

EXAMINATION AND PROGNOSIS
If you treat a man for ball-like tumors on his chest and you find they have spread on his chest, and if you put your hand on his chest on those tumors and you find it very cold, with no warmth in it, and your hand finds they have no granularity, and they do not make water or create drops of water but are ball-like to your hand, then you say about him: "One who has ball-like tumors: an ailment I will fight with."

TREATMENT
It is nothing. If you find ball-like tumors in any limb of a man, you should treat him according to these practices.

EXPLANATION
As for "ball-like tumors on his chest," it means there are swellings on his chest, big, spread out, and hard, which when touched are like when a ball of bandages is touched, similar to a fresh fenugreek pod when it is hard and cool under your hand, like when those swellings that are on his chest are touched.

CASE 46. A CHEST BLISTER (15,20–16,16)

TITLE
Practices for a raised blister in his chest.

EXAMINATION AND PROGNOSIS
If you treat a man for a raised blister in his chest and you find a very big eruption has risen on his chest,

NOTE
11. The physician makes a clear distinction between an abscess (Case 39) and the firm (solid, neoplastic) growth described here. He varies his treatment accordingly, but it was most likely ineffectual.

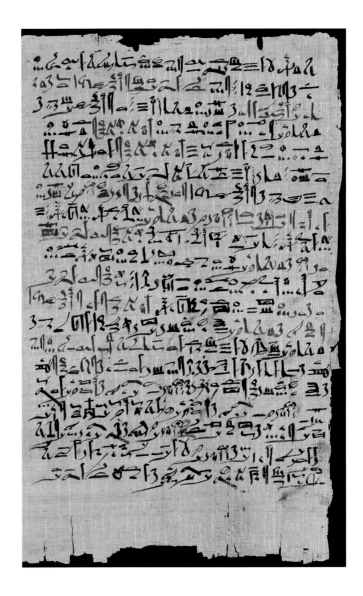

clear like water under your hand, and they have made something clammy of aspect but their faces have not reddened, then you say about him: "One who has a raised blister in his chest: an ailment I will handle with cool media (applied) to that blister that is in his chest."

TREATMENT

Sḫt fruit, natron, and *qzntj* mineral, ground and bandaged on it; (or) calcite powder, *qzntj* mineral, builder's mortar, and water, ground and bandaged on it.

If those cool media are resisted, then you would delay a prescription for him until all the water that is in the blister goes down and treat him with treatment for a wound, with media for drawing heat from the mouth of a wound in his chest: acacia leaves, sycamore leaves, water, date palm leaves, gall of oxen, and grass, bandaged on it. Then you make him an astringent in his chest: powder of malachite, colocynth, cedar, fat, oil, northern salt, and ibex fat, bandaged on it. Then you make him poultices: poppy seeds, flax seeds, and sycamore, ground and put on it.

EXPLANATIONS

As for "a raised blister in his chest," it means there is a big swelling on the injury that is in his chest, soft like water under the hand.

As for "their aspect is clammy," it means their skin is not feverish.

As for "there is no redness on it," it means there is nothing red on it.

CASE 47. A GAPING WOUND ABOVE THE SHOULDER BLADE (16,16–17,15)

TITLE

Practices for a gaping wound in his shoulder blade area.

EXAMINATION AND PROGNOSIS

If you treat a man for a gaping wound in his shoulder blade area, whose flesh has been removed and whose sides are separated, and he suffers from drainage in his shoulder blade, ⟨you have to⟩ say (*mistake for* probe) his wound. Should you find its gap shifted and its sides pushed away from his wound like the unrolling of a ball of linen, and it is hard for him to lift his arm from it, you have to fasten its gap for him with thread. Then you say about him:

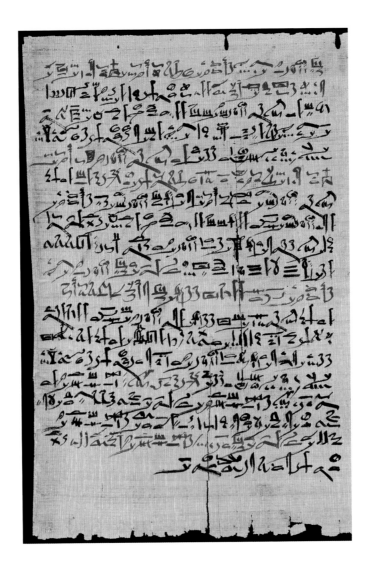

"One who has a gaping wound in his shoulder blade area, whose flesh has been removed and whose sides are separated, and he suffers from drainage in his shoulder blade: an ailment I will handle."

TREATMENT
You have to bandage him with fresh meat the first day. If you find that wound opened up and its threads loosened, fasten its gap for him with lengths of cloth on that gap and treat him afterward (with) an oil and honey dressing every day until he gets well.

If you find a wound whose flesh has been removed and whose sides are separated in any limb of a man, you should evaluate him according to these practices.

ALTERNATIVE EXAMINATION AND PROGNOSIS
But if you find that wound with its flesh having taken warmth in that wound in his shoulder blade area, and that wound is inflamed and opened up, with its threads loosened, then you put your hand on him. Should you find warmth issuing from the mouth of his wound at your hand, with drops that fall from it cool like the water of currants, then you say about him: "One who has a gaping wound in his shoulder blade area, which is inflamed, and he is feverish from it: an ailment I will fight with."

ALTERNATIVE TREATMENT
And when you find that man feverish, and that wound is inflamed, you should not bandage him. He is to be put down on his bed until the time of his injury has passed. And when his fever has been shortened, and warmth shoots away from the mouth of his wound, you should treat him afterward (with) an oil and honey dressing every day until he gets well.

CASE 48. A PULLED VERTEBRA (17,15–19)

TITLE
Practices for a pull of a vertebra of his back.

EXAMINATION AND PROGNOSIS
If you treat (a man for) a pull in a vertebra of his back, then you say to him: "Please extend your legs and contract them." He has to extend them and he has to contract them immediately because it is hard for him to do (it) from the vertebra of his back that he suffers from. Then you say about him: "One who has a pull in a vertebra of his back: an ailment I will handle."

TREATMENT
You have to put him stretched out. You have to make for him

(end of recto)

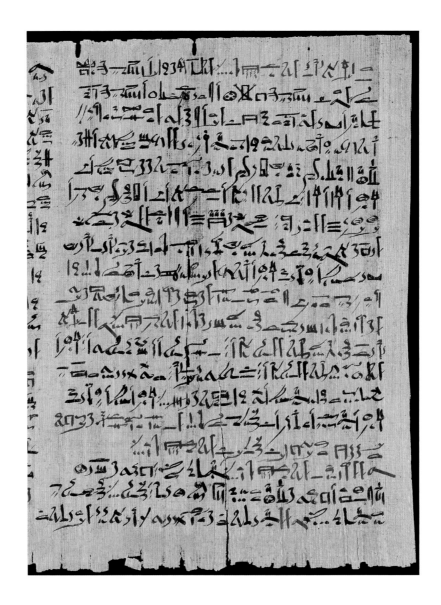

SPELL 1. AGAINST PESTILENTIAL AIR (V. 1,1–10)

Spell for barring the air of a disease year.

Oh, Flame-in-His-face, at the fore of the Akhet! Speak to Foremost-of-Neith-Town, who makes firm Osiris at the fore of the land. Nekhbet, who separates the land from the sky for her father, come and tie two plumes behind me, that I may live and become sound. For I am that white one atop the elder god in Heliopolis: the second is Isis, the third is Nephthys, and I am after for you. Grasper of the great (crown), Sekhmet's son; Controlling Powers' Controller, the night-demon's son; Wrathful, son of Hathor, lady of the Red Crown—who swells the rivers as you row Nu and sail in the Dayboat! You have saved me from every bitterness, etc., of this year in the wind of every bad air. Horus, Horus, the sound one of Sekhmet, be all around my flesh for life!

To be recited over 2 feathers of a vulture, spread over a man and put as his protection against any place he might walk in. It is the year's protection; it is a bitterness repeller in a year of disease.

SPELL 2. AGAINST PESTILENTIAL AIR (V. 1,11–16)

Another for barring air of the bitterness of the night-demons, those of smallness, Sekhmet's messengers.

Retreat, night-demons! Winds shall not reach me until those who pass by for tempest pass by me. I am Horus, who passed by Sekhmet's infection. Horus, Horus, sound one of Sekhmet! I am the unique one, Bastet's son. I shall not die for you (goddess).

To be recited by a man with a stick of *dz* wood in his arm, as he goes out and goes around his house. He cannot die because of a disease year.

SPELL 3. AGAINST PESTILENCE (V. 1,17–19)

Another protection for a disease year.

I am the abomination that comes from Dep, Meskhenet that comes from Heliopolis. People, gods, spirits, and dead, be far from me! I am abomination.

SPELL 4. AGAINST FEVER (V. 1,19–V. 2,2)

Another.

I am sound in the path of those who pass by. So, shall I be hit while sound?

I have seen the great tempest. You fever, don't push into me! I am one who escaped from tempest. Be far from me!

Bastet from (entering) a man's house, which a man should say in the year's oaths.

SPELL 5. AGAINST MENTAL AND EMOTIONAL DISORDERS (V. 2,2–14)

Copy of another.

Hysteria, hysteria, you should not acquire this my mind or this my heart for Sekhmet, you should not acquire my liver for Osiris or anyone at all in the hidden thing in Pe at the dawn when Horus's eye allots the implement against my mat: any male spirit, any female spirit, any male dead, any female dead, the form of any animal, one whom the crocodile has acquired or the snake has bitten, one condemned to the knife or who has passed away on his bed, the night-demons of the year's wake or contents. Horus, Horus, the sound one of Sekhmet, (be) all (around my) flesh for life!

To be recited over Sekhmet, Bastet, Osiris, or Nehebkau. To be written in myrrh on a strip of fine linen, and given to a man at his neck: "Donkeys, those of Neferi, or a green-fronted mallard are not to be allowed to enter to me, for the life-protection of Neith is around me, she who precedes the one who escaped sowing." (It is a way of) stopping

SPELL 6. AGAINST A SWALLOWED FLY (V. 2,14–18)

Spell for cleansing a fly.

The mouth of this man, etc., under (the care of) my fingers is the mouth of a milk calf as it comes from the belly of his mother. This insect that has entered this belly of his has entered and come forth from him alive, issuing forth to the ground as excrement or as effluent, without injuring his belly. It has come forth from him as his effluent, allotted to the Horizon god.

SPELL 7. AGAINST DISEASE (V. 2,18–V. 3,8)

Spell for cleansing anything from disease.

Your messengers have gone up in flames, Sekhmet. Your night demons have retreated, Bastet. The year has not passed for

VERSO, COLUMN 3

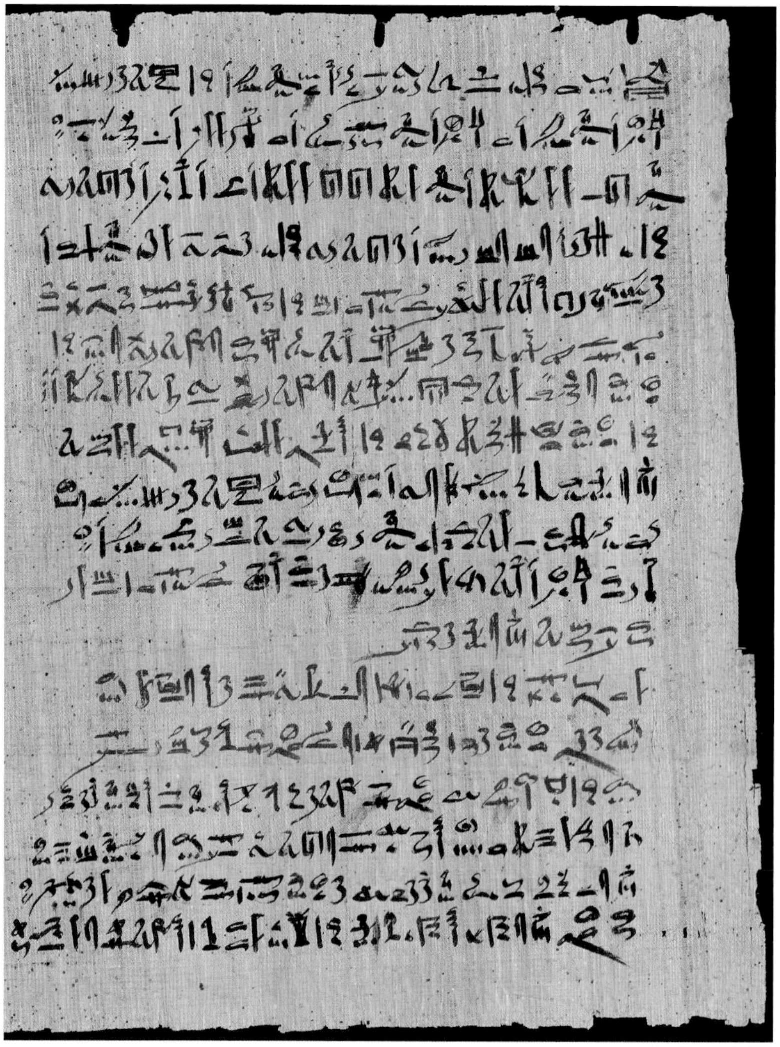

tempest against me. Your winds shall not reach me. I am Horus over Sekhmet's night-demons. I am your Horus, Sekhmet. I am your Unique One, Wadjet. I shall not die for you; I shall not die for you. I am Ululator. I am Jubilator. Bastet's son, don't come down on me. You in disarray, don't come down on me, don't come near me. I am the King within his glaucoma.

A man should say this spell over the front of a fresh flower, tied on a piece of *dz* wood and bound with a strip of first-class linen, and passed over the thing. The disease will be driven off and the passage of night-demons over anything eaten as well as over beds will be barred.

SPELL 8. AGAINST DISEASE (V. 3,8–12)

Another.

Daisies are on me, your followers' abomination (Sekhmet). Your infection shall exempt me, the trap of your bird-snare shall exempt me. I am the one of your birds who got away. Horus, Horus, the sound one of Sekhmet, be all around my flesh for life.

A man should say this spell after he has put daisies in his hand.

PRESCRIPTION 1. FOR MENSTRUAL PROBLEMS (V. 3,13–V. 4,3)

If you examine a woman suffering in her stomach and for whom nothing comes as menstruation, and you find something in the upper side of her navel, then you say about her: "It is a blockage of blood at her womb."

You have to make her 1 ⅓ cup of *wȝm* plants, ½ cup of oil, and 2 ½ cups of sweet beer, cooked and drunk for 4 days, as well as making her something to make the blood descend: cedar oil, caraway seeds, galena, and sweet myrrh, made into a compound and her vagina smeared with it many, many times. You have to add aardwolf-ear plants to oil. After she begins bleeding, you have to rub

VERSO, COLUMN 4

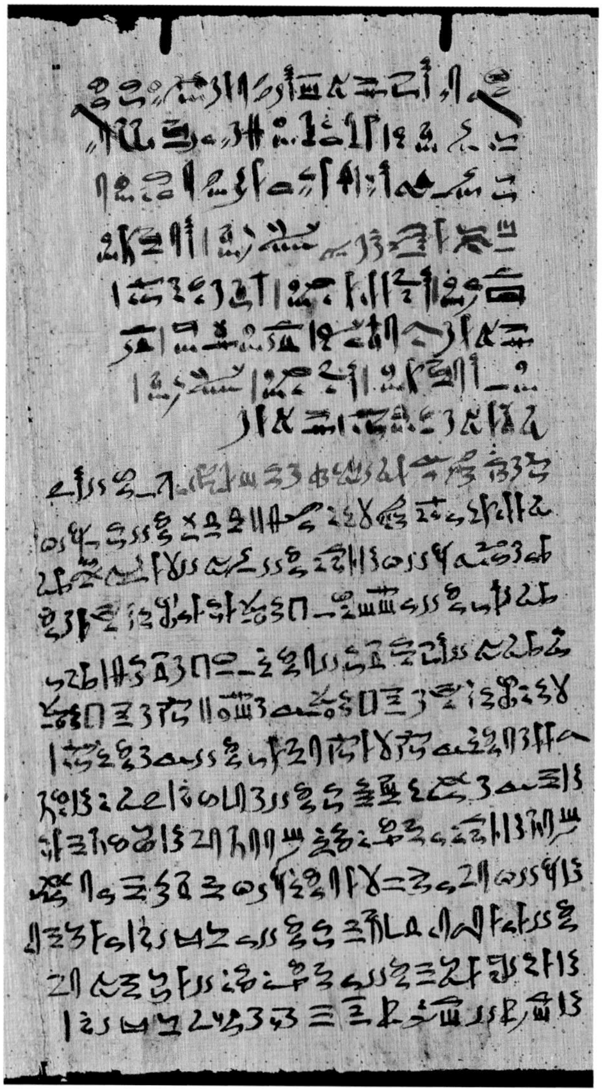

her and smear her pelvis with it many, many times, and the fumes of it are to be made to enter her flesh.

PRESCRIPTION 2. FOR RENEWING THE SKIN (V. 4,3–6)

Prescription for reversion of the skin.

Honey 1, red natron 1, northern salt 1, ground into a compound and smeared on.

PRESCRIPTION 3. FOR REJUVENATING THE FACE (V. 4,6–8)

Another for rejuvenating the face.

Calcite powder 1, powder of natron 1, northern salt 1, honey 1, mixed into a compound and smeared on.

PRESCRIPTION 4. A REJUVENATING POTION (V. 4,8–V. 5,10)

Beginning of the scroll of making an old man into a youth.

One has to get a great many bitter almonds, comparable to 3 bushels. They have to be pulverized and put in the sunlight. After they have dried completely, they have to be threshed like threshing grain. They have to be winnowed until only the kernels of them remain. As for all that comes from this, it has to be measured, as well as sieving the chaff of the threshing floor with a sieve. Measure likewise all those kernels that have come out. Make into 2 parts: one, of those kernels, and the other, of the chaff. Make one part equal to the other.

They have to be set as a compound in water and made into a soft dough. They have to be put in a new pot on the fire and cooked completely and adequately. You will know they have cooked (adequately) by the water evaporating and by their drying out until they are like dry chaff, without moisture in it.

They have to be taken out. When they have cooled, they have to be put in a jug to wash them in the river. They have to be washed adequately. One will know they have been washed (adequately) by one tasting the taste of the water that is in the jug

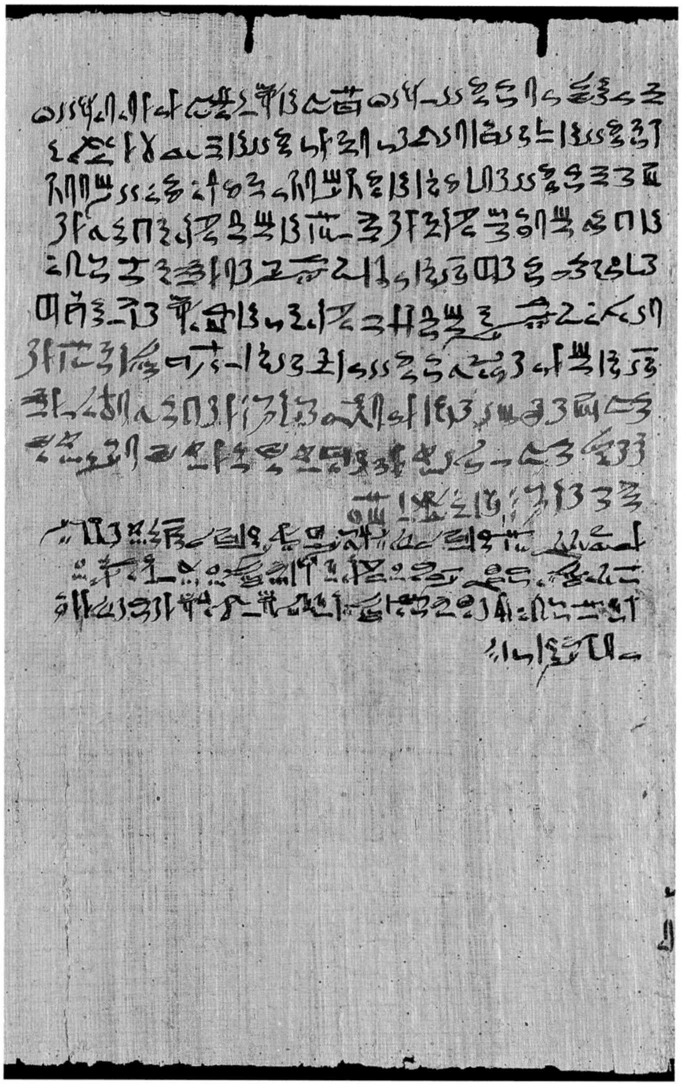

without any bitterness to it.

It has to be put in the sunlight spread out on the cloth of a washerman. When it has dried, it has to be ground on a grinding stone. It has to be set in water and made like soft dough. It has to be put in a pot on the fire and cooked adequately. One will know (it) has cooked (adequately) by beads of oil coming from it.

A man shall keep ladling the oil that comes from it with a scoop. It is to be put in a jar after it has congealed into (a substance like) clay, its congealing having been smoothed and thickened. Ladle this oil to be put on the linen cover on the upper side of this jar. Afterward, it should be put in a jar of fine stone.

Anoint a man with it. It is something that repels a cold from the head. If the body is wiped with it, what results is rejuvenation of the skin and repelling of wrinkles, any age spots, any sign of old age, and any fever that may be in the body. (Proved) good a million times.

PRESCRIPTION 5. FOR HEMORRHOIDS (V. 5,11–14)

If you see a man suffering from his rear when he stands up or sits down, and suffering very greatly from contractions of his legs, you have to make him a prescription of oil, "great-protection" resin, and leaves of acacia, ground, smoothed, and cooked into a compound. A strip of fine linen is to be anointed with it and put in the anus for his immediate recovery.